OVERHAUL
YOUR
CAREER

SEVEN TIPS FOR RESTORING
YOUR CLASSIC MODEL FOR NEW ROADS

CHRIS FONTANELLA

ILLUMIFY
MEDIA.COM

Overhaul Your Career

Copyright © 2025 by Chris Fontanella

Published by

Illumify Media Global

www.IllumifyMedia.com

"Let's bring your book to life!"

Paperback ISBN: 978-1-964251-35-6

Cover design by Debbie Lewis

Printed in the United States of America

CONTENTS

FOREWORD

I HAVE HAD THE PRIVILEGE of knowing and working alongside Chris for many years. His career is a testament not only to his longevity as a highly accomplished executive but also to the breadth of industries, roles, and challenges he has navigated with remarkable success. *Overhaul Your Career* is a reflection of the tenacity, adaptability, and rigor that have defined his professional journey. In a world evolving at an unprecedented pace—what some are calling the next industrial revolution—the ability to adapt and thrive has never been more critical.

Overhaul Your Career serves as both a timely and indispensable roadmap for individuals seeking to extend their professional success into what Chris refers to as the "last third" of their careers. It challenges the notion that career longevity is solely about stamina or youth, offering instead a perspective grounded in resilience, curiosity, and lifelong learning.

If you find yourself in the later stages of your career, don't let the absence of youth feel like a barrier. Today's organizations don't just need fresh talent; they need employees who can think critically, adapt swiftly, and leverage technology effectively. While younger generations may seem more attuned to technology, the truth is that adaptability and a willingness to learn are far more valuable in this era of constant innovation. Many modern tools and platforms are designed to be accessible to non-technical users, making it possible for anyone, regardless of age, to harness their power—provided they approach them with curiosity and a learning mindset.

Artificial intelligence, in particular, is poised to reshape every industry, role, and level of the workforce. As we stand at the cusp of this new era, those with a wealth of career experience are uniquely positioned to combine their hard-earned skills with emerging technologies. This blend of expertise and innovation is a powerful asset for individuals and organizations alike.

Chris's book is both a guide and an inspiration for seasoned professionals who are ready to embrace change, stay curious, and redefine what success looks like in this transformative age. With the right mindset and a commitment to learning, you can enjoy a fulfilling and impactful career—no matter your age.

—Mairtini Ni Dhomhnaill
Founder of Countsy

*"Most people go to their graves
with their music still inside them."*

—*Oliver Wendell Holmes*

INTRODUCTION

"WHERE DID THE TIME GO?" That's what my eighty-seven-year-old dad said one day as my family looked at pictures from my parents' dating life and early marital years. It's a question that seldom, if ever, gets answered. The band Chicago offered a response—albeit by asking another question: "Does Anybody Really Know What Time It Is?"

Maybe you're like me and looking back over your career, wondering where the time went. You might also be starting to think about what to do with the remaining career road ahead of you.

Many people I know are in the last third of their working lives. They are long past the commencement of their careers when they were aspiring young professionals eager to explore a world of opportunities—the chance of a lifetime. They're also beyond the middle stage, the period when years of experience accumulate.

If you can relate and find yourself questioning what's next, especially if you lack a plan, allow me to put a bug in your ear: the starting gun has gone off, and you're still at the gate. You're behind schedule. As a Japanese proverb says, "The best time to plant a tree was twenty years ago; the next best time is now." In other words, what are you waiting for? Get going.

The back end of your career can be an interesting, somewhat strange time. Honestly, I feel a bit lost—maybe you do too. Decisions about your career can be difficult in general, but they seem even more challenging when you're acutely aware that more of the road is behind you than ahead. Should your main focus be making money, given that your primary earning years are dwindling? Or should you prioritize happiness, even if it means a lower salary for your services? At this stage in your life, how should you define career aspirations? What should be the aim of the latter stage of your career?

It seems to me that whatever you choose to do, it should at least be meaningful and purposeful. Wouldn't it be wonderful if, after all these years of work, you found your sweet spot—what Susan Cain defines as "the place where you're optimally stimulated"?[1] At this point, perhaps more than at any other time in your career, shouldn't work be more than a chorus of monotonous chores or *just* a job? Shouldn't it be a time when you engage in "an activity that will make [your life] make sense,"[2] when you're no longer working just to make a buck? By now, there should be harmony between your occupation and your sense of calling, right?

If you've picked up this book, you may be eyeing the end of your employment life; while you're not quite at the end, you're heading toward it.

The way I see it—a perspective drawn from over thirty years of finding jobs for people—the start of a career should be like an adventure, filled with excitement and enthusiasm. Sure, an entry-level role comes with its fair share of drudgery, but you have to start somewhere, and the bottom is as good a place as any. Even so, the initial phase of a career burns with limitless potential and infinite possibilities: while you never fully know where your first job might take you, within it lie the seeds of all your career could become.

The midpoint of a career can burn brightly too—or at least it should. By this time, employees have been "at it" for a while. They've reached a certain level of experience, and that experience has presumably made them proficient in what they do. They're in their prime, firing on all cylinders, so to speak. Been there, done that.

Eventually, however, you move beyond these stages and enter the last third of your career—the "back nine," the latter stage, "the last chapter before death,"[3] what some deem a less-than-radiant phase of employment. Even so, regardless of how this stage is labeled, reflecting on "the end" allows you to identify any necessary adaptations to further develop your career with renewed purpose.

Aging, including in the workplace, doesn't always feel good. Or, as Steve Lopez says in a *Los Angeles Times* article titled "As Years Pass, the Perks of Old Age Do Add Up," "Aging has its drawbacks, if you hadn't noticed."[4] Having years of work under your belt can be both a blessing and a curse: being a seasoned professional has its advantages—almost everyone sees experience as an asset—but it also means you're no longer the young kid on the block. That said, if you've reached this phase, you've invested a significant amount of time to get here. If a career spans 90,000 to 125,000 hours,[5] as some have calculated, then you've already logged a large percentage of that time.

Including my money-making endeavors as a kid—mowing lawns in the summer, shoveling driveways in the winter, delivering newspapers year-round, working at a local pizzeria, and running my window-washing business called Spot-Free Enterprises—I have worked a total of forty-five years. And I'm not even sixty yet. (It should be noted, however, that those employment opportunities were not standard forty-hour-per-week jobs. They were odd jobs, side hustles, and part-time roles to make some "scratch.")

As I got older and dove deeper into the working world, I served as a full-time minister of a church and a part-time manager at a bank. During that time, I was also working toward my master's degree in theological studies. Years later, I became a business development manager at a staffing company. On Friday and Saturday nights, I also worked at a comedy club to supplement my income. Ultimately, I went on to found two accounting and finance consulting businesses: BF Consultants and Encore Professionals Group. (How a person with a master's in theological studies ends up starting two businesses that identify jobs for CPAs and MBAs makes for an interesting story. You can read more about that in my other books.)

All this to say, like you, I have recorded my fair share of work hours, filled out plenty of time sheets, and have likely worked closer to 125,000 hours than 90,000. Like you, I am in the last third of my career.

Because I find jobs for people for a living, my network often refers candidates to me. Most of these introductions are made via email and typically include an attached resume, which offers clues as to the career phase these job seekers are in. Given the caliber of candidates I typically work with, most are either in or nearing the later stages of their careers.

As a courtesy, I call each person. Their backstories are usually similar: the company they worked for or currently work for has been sold, acquired, or downsized. Sometimes their job has been outsourced to another state or country, or the company has decided to "head in a different direction," whatever that means. These scenarios, and others like them, have led to the candidate losing—or being about to lose—their job.

—

What I have found in each of these situations is this: you learn more about the candidate's true feelings regarding their circumstances from what they are *not* saying. When you have interviewed a host of job seekers, like I have, you learn to hear the unspoken.

These "older" candidates, now on the hunt for a new gig, are eager to discuss their career experiences, employment history, areas of expertise and leadership skills, the projects they've managed, and even how they helped the company letting them go merge into the acquiring company that decided not to retain them. What they are less comfortable sharing, however, is how they feel about being out of a job at their age. Most choose not to address it, though occasionally someone might say, "Look, I know the reality of my situation. I'm no spring chicken."

After listening to them, I can tell they still "have it." They're still on top of their game; their skills are top-notch. When it comes to their vast career expertise, as the saying goes, they've forgotten more than most will ever learn. Yet in light of being let go, they now wonder if another company will want them at their age. They're starting to grapple with questions like, *What's next for me career-wise? Are there still opportunities for someone like me?* and *Will another company pay me what I've been making—what I feel I'm worth?* At a deeper level, they're expressing a desire to continue contributing, to feel valued, and to maintain a sense of purpose in their lives. And as strange as it may seem to some, they believe work offers that.

Sometimes these work scenarios are forced upon us. We seldom have control over decisions made by an organization, yet we are impacted by them and left to figure out what to do next.

Years back, for example, I worked for a bank that decided to sell the division I was part of to a bank based in Minnesota. The job was mine if I wanted it, but it wouldn't be in sunny Southern California where I lived. Events like divestitures and acquisitions—and others like them—happen to companies all the time. It's unsettling when they leave you displaced, but it's even more daunting if it happens later in your career, when you feel you have less career road ahead. But such events aren't the only reason we start considering how much career road is left. Often, our own thoughts and feelings prompt us to do so as we naturally begin to wonder about what we perceive to be our remaining time in our vocation.

Some fortunate souls truly enjoy—and have always enjoyed—their work. They've known from day one what they were meant to do vocationally and have been doing it their whole career. Dr. Kent Weeks, archeologist extraordinaire, is one such person. By his own account, he knew from the age of eight that he wanted to be an archaeologist and went on to build an illustrious lifelong career in the field. On a smaller scale, due to her age, my daughter Geena also fits this profile. At a young age, she realized her life must revolve around music, one way or another, and ever since, she's been "all about it."

People like this feel confident in their career path and see no need to change direction, content to continue on their chosen road. That's commendable. However, as time rolls on, even such individuals will need to adapt and explore other avenues within their field of interest to sustain growth and success, as well as make accommodations due to changes in desire, capability, and circumstances. (Dr. Weeks's career adjustments—the twists and turns of his employment journey—are detailed in my book *Jump-Start Your Career*).

Few employees want to keep doing the "same old thing" over and over again. At a certain point, many begin to explore variations on their career's theme. They "branch off" a bit and, in the process, avoid a "same sh*t, different day" existence.

Most of us, however, fumbled around until we found a career—or maybe it found us. And by the time we reach the latter stage of our career, many of us are over it. We've grown tired of doing what we've been doing and are ready for something new. We find ourselves at an impasse but are clueless about how to step over the threshold into a renewed sense of self and purpose. Timothy Butler hits the nail on the head when he says we need a "dynamic dislodging" and a "reinvigorated role"[6]—something that jars us loose from our warm work womb and thrusts us into a new and meaningful, albeit unfamiliar, world.

Maybe you've reached the highest rung on the corporate ladder. There are no more positions above you, and at the same time, you no longer find your job rewarding. Or maybe you feel you just have nothing left to offer your employer. Perhaps you feel pulled to pursue other interests, to chase a dream that, until now, has been dormant in your heart. Or maybe you feel gripped by a feeling of ennui, leaving you uncertain and unenthusiastic about your career. You can't quite explain it; you just know you're not thrilled about it anymore.

You can find a plethora of information and advice on the latter stage of your career—how one might feel going through it, what options it affords, and more. Bookstores, blogs, and podcast babblers offer much information on the subject of career development. This book merely adds to the heap of material on the topic. Much of it can prove beneficial. But . . .

Even if it contains helpful information, it's meaningless unless you put it into action. Application is key.

Every phase of your career, including its final stage, requires you to take responsibility for the direction in which you steer your career vehicle. Personal accountability is the foundation of every noteworthy career.

By all means, listen to others—read their books and blogs, and listen to their podcasts. Consider what they have to say. Career achievements and advancements, regardless of the stage you find yourself in, are seldom solo efforts. The counsel of others may point you in a direction worth exploring; a piece of wisdom they offer could lead you right where you are meant to be. So don't dismiss the advice and assistance of others out of hand; it may prove invaluable. Just remember, the ultimate decision about which road to take rests with you. You choose the direction in which to drive your career vehicle.

Late-stage career professionals can experience feelings of ambivalence, reluctance, and vacillation. Mixed emotions are common. Many also feel overwhelmed by a loss of purpose and stymied by aimlessness. It's not uncommon to hesitate and waver when deciding which direction to take; you may often feel uncertain about which road to follow. Even seasoned employees go through career "whiteout" conditions, when they have zero visibility and are blind to what lies ahead.

These feelings tend to give rise to questions that only the individual can answer: Where can I take my career from here? What does my employment future hold? Can I convert my years of experience in one industry into a completely different one? Are my skills transferable? Do I still have something to offer an employer, society, the world? Are my years of experience an asset or a deficit? Are my gifts and talents still of value? Do I have a second, third, fourth, or fifth career act in me—an encore performance?

Despite such questions and the bombardment of doubts and fears, you still have more to offer. The motor may be older, but it still warms up.

Nearing or entering the latter stage of your career does not mean you are at its end; approaching the end is not the same as being at the end. Ending one phase actually puts you at the beginning of another. And one mustn't surrender to the notion that the last third of one's career cannot be as good as—or even better than—the phases that preceded it. It can be, as long as you are willing to deliberate over what you want it to look like and take the time to explore the various opportunities available to someone of your "stature."

Transition points, such as entering the latter stage of your career, call for reflection. They beckon us to think and contemplate, to look thoughtfully both backward and forward. As Mary Catherine Bateson says in her thought-provoking book *Composing a Further Life: The Age of Active Wisdom,* "Composing a further life involves thinking about the entire process of composing a life . . . It involves looking with new eyes at what has been lived so far and making choices that show the whole process in a new light and that offer a sense of completion and fulfillment."[7]

D. Michael Lindsay calls these transformational shifts "hinge moments." He describes them as opportunities that afford us "the chance to open [or close] doors to various pathways of our lives."[8] His point, like that of Bateson, suggests that a transitional moment—a "crossroad" perhaps—has the potential to connect preceding career movements to those that have yet to occur. These moments hold the potential to bridge the inflection points in your work life.

The importance of these hinge moments cannot be overstated. They can either propel you forward or, if you choose to do nothing, leave you stalled in your career journey. This is why reflection is an appropriate course of action: careful thought must be given to the steps you take next.

Consider this: at this point, your career vehicle is like a classic car. It has traveled more miles than you may care to remember. It may even require special handling—after all, this is not a brand-new car fresh off the lot. Regardless, it's capable of getting you from point A to point B. The car still holds value—no doubt about it. (If you've followed my advice in *Tune Up Your Career*, its engine continues to function at an optimal level.)

Nevertheless, age-related issues are starting to show.

Vintage vehicles require repairs, new parts, and perhaps even a fresh coat of paint. The older the ride, the more miles traveled, and the more wear and tear you can expect. The same is true of career vehicles. Their "older" occupants have been driving miles and miles up and down Corporate America's highways and the streets of the working world. As a result, their ride needs servicing to address the inevitable deterioration and depreciation. No offense, but as they say, if the shoe (or driver's seat) fits . . .

The road takes its toll; there's no shame in admitting it. Most cars that have been on the road a while have their fair share of damages and dings—and that's just the outside. Parts under the hood are also subject to wear and should be examined too; the steering, fuel, and cooling systems, as well as the driveshaft and engine, need to be checked.

Eventually, every vehicle, especially older ones, needs a little TLC. So if you've been on your employment journey for forty years or more, chances are your career vehicle is overdue for repair, renovation, and renewal. In a word, it needs to be overhauled. It's essential if you expect it to remain functional. But remember, no matter how much work you put into it, the vehicle will never be brand new again: a classic car—any car—is only original once.

However, it can be enduringly operational.

To that end, *Overhaul Your Career: Seven Tips for Restoring Your Classic Model for New Roads* aims to provide guidance on repairing, renovating, and renewing your career vehicle to its best functional state at this stage of your professional journey.

Among other things, you will be encouraged to redefine your idea of retirement, reclaim your inner rebel, remember who you are to reprise yourself, reimagine employment, reminisce without lingering too long on the past, and replace broken or faulty parts.

If you didn't know much about Alecia Beth Hart Moore before her *60 Minutes* interview, you've learned plenty after it aired on June 9, 2024.

Known professionally as Pink, Moore has quite a story to tell. Despite singing gospel songs as a kid, she had a troubled home life. Her dad was an alcoholic, and she clashed often, as daughters do, with her mother. Her teenage years were also problematic—she was the kid other parents did *not* want their own kid hanging out with. Pink attributes this to being a "punk" with a "mouth" and a chip on her shoulder. On top of it all, she got into—and sold—drugs, and eventually overdosed. In a nutshell, her life was, as she states, "off the rails."

Just weeks after her overdose, she landed a record deal, at which time, she was asked to take etiquette classes in the hopes of curbing her personality. That deal—and the classes—didn't last; she couldn't be something she was not. So she went solo.

Her music, a mix of rock and pop, hit home with fans. Her second studio album, *Missundazstood,* hit the market and sold fifteen million copies. She's been off to the races ever since.

Despite her success, she has not stopped pushing ahead. At forty-four, she's planning her next move: a Las Vegas residency. (She has also branched off and is a vintner.) She continues to demand more of herself and is determined to fight time. She sees no reason to stop. As she says, "Why can't we ride until the wheels fall off? That's what I plan on doing."[9]

That's the attitude I am proposing you adopt as you navigate your career vehicle through the last third of it. In other words, prepare to go the distance.

How one develops and builds their vocational life—from beginning to end—is uniquely personal. No two are alike: mine is distinct to me, just as yours is to you. Careers are, to use a Latin phrase, *sui generis*, "of its own kind." How I navigate the later stage of mine will differ from the way you choose to cruise through yours. And that's as it should be— the most exemplary careers are always those that are uniquely personalized.

No hard and fast rules exist when it comes to this. Keep that in mind as you read what follows. What works for me or someone else may not work for you. So please use the following material in a way that best suits you. As they say, eat the meat and spit out the bones. Apply what you find valuable and forget the rest.

1
LET'S CALL IT A DAY

RETIRE THE IDEA OF RETIREMENT

IT WAS NINE A.M. ON a Tuesday morning. My workout accomplished, I decided to hit the sauna. It was packed.

Nine guys—most on the larger side—had crowded themselves into the ten-by-ten steam box. That's one hundred square feet for eight overweight men—a category which includes me—and one scrawny guy. It felt like, and somewhat smelled like, a sardine can, except only one inhabitant, the scrawny guy, qualified as a sardine. (The word *sardine* means "small fish." When it matures and gets larger, they are then called herring. So, since most of us were large, it would be more accurate to say I was in a herring tin, not a sardine can.)

Anyway, out of the steamy mist, one man called to his buddy, who, if I were to venture a guess, appeared to be sixty years old, and said, "Hey! Isn't today your first day of retirement?" In a thunderous, Martin Luther King Jr.–like fashion, he replied, "Yesterday was! Free at last. Free at last. Thank God Almighty, I am free at last."

His outburst was met with a chorus of congratulations. I mean, what kind of herring would you be if you didn't congratulate a fellow herring on his retirement? But his exclamation made me wonder what he did for a living and how he felt about his career before retirement. Based on his emancipation proclamation, whatever he did, he must not have enjoyed it much. It sounded like he'd been swimming upstream his whole life or he'd been stuck in an inescapable tide pool and had finally put an end to it all. It sounded as if his career had lacked significance. *Had he enjoyed his years of employment,* I wondered. Unlikely. *Had he built a noteworthy career?* Probably not.

"All too often we work because we must, and we make the best of a bad situation," says Sam Keen in his book *Fire in the Belly: On Being a Man.*[1] But one's work life should be more than that and not merely a means to an end. Nor should it be "an endless grind and waste of hours spent trying to white-knuckle our way through the misery of it all until the weekend [or retirement] comes."[2] If "finding one's role is tantamount to finding one's voice," as Alan Briskin writes in his thought-provoking book *The Stirring of Soul in the Workplace,* then it appears the man in the sauna never figured out how to make his job an expression of himself.[3]

As far as I could tell, regardless of what he did for a living, my fellow herring's work life seemed to lack a sense of calling and purpose. For him, *not* working had greater value *than* working. He reached a point where he was "over it" and ready to call it a day . . . for good.

Doubtful he's alone.

Countless people feel this way about work . . . about their career. Hence why they adopt the same attitude as their career approaches its end. The dignity that comes from work and its significance has seeped out; its meaningfulness has oozed away. So retirement—what some see as their golden opportunity to withdraw from an active work life—starts to sound appealing. Like the boisterous herring in the steam room, these individuals have reached a point where they are eager to remove themselves from and swear off work altogether.

But if a career is a *lifelong* journey, as I believe it to be, then retirement, in the sense described above, would best be retired. You'd be better off putting it out of your mind, laying it to rest, and not entertaining it.

A career hero—someone who maintains personal accountability for their life of employment from its beginning to its end—does not subscribe to the traditional definition of retirement. Instead of the latter stage of one's career being the time to detach from the working world for good, the career superstar opts to view it as an opportunity to segue into something different, something redefined and recast. It's his or her time to mull over new ways to contribute and participate.

Jo Ann Jenkins, CEO of AARP, gets at this in the foreword to *Work Reimagined: Uncover Your Calling*, when she says, "We need to get to the point where we are no longer defined by the old expectations of what we should do or should not do at a certain age, and that means we need to reimagine our lives so we can be open to joy and fulfillment throughout our days. After all, it is not really about aging; it is about living."[4]

Retirement does not mean you have to turn off the engine, relinquish your seat behind the steering wheel, and hand over the keys of your career vehicle. There may be a time for that much further down the road, but now is not that time.

At least one other option exists. You can find another gear. In a word: downshift. A slower pace—one reality of late-stage work life and aging—is to be preferred over being immobile. Slowing down is fine; just don't stop.

The innate desire you have to convey who you are through your work will be present on some level until your dying day. Humans are not wired to be useless and without a sense of purpose. What is required of you, then, is to find the right gear to best give expression to that drive inherent within you, no matter what stage of the journey you find yourself.

Christine McVie, Rock and Roll Hall of Famer, joined Fleetwood Mac around 1970. She wrote or cowrote many Mac favorites, including "Don't Stop," "Little Lies," "Say You Love Me," and "Hold Me." After an almost thirty-year stint with the band, she retired and moved to England's countryside.

Who could blame her? It's not easy being a famous rock-and-roller; studio work is demanding, and touring schedules are grueling, especially so for Christine, a reluctant traveler due to a fear of flying.[5] Toss in drug use and the turmoil of strained relationships, and you can understand the difficulties an occupation like this presents. (The on-again, off-again relationship of Stevie Nicks, the band's singer, and Leslie Buckingham, the band's guitarist, is *still* fodder for journalists, and Christine's relationship with bass player, John McVie—a relationship that ended in divorce—also made headlines.)

No wonder she longed for more peaceful terrain.

Years after she had stepped away, Mick Fleetwood, the band's drummer, asked her to (re)join him and her ex-husband for a music session at his restaurant in Lahaina, Hawaii, Fleetwood's on Front Street. To assuage her aviation-related fears, Mick said he would be willing to accompany her on the flight to Hawaii. Christine accepted the offer and sat in on the session.

After a period of reflection, says music critic Mikael Wood, Christine concluded that by *not* playing music, she had neglected a part of herself. She realized she had "given up" and stopped "paying respect to [her] own gift."[6] Her choice to retreat into the security and privacy of England's farmland deprived her of one thing the latter stage of a career can offer—an opportunity to honor and share your gifts and talents. Her story makes me wonder what we rob from others when we decide to excuse ourselves (i.e., retire) from an active life of work, when we decide to "call it day" career wise.

To be clear, I am not suggesting anything is wrong or amiss if, at this phase in your career, you want to slow down, stop to smell the roses, or even step away for what Matthew McConaughey calls a "self-induced hiatus."[7] If you have reached that point, and if your financial ducks are in a row and allow for that, then have at it—enjoy the fruits of your labor. You've earned it. Indulge yourself in the freedom, time, and space that this period affords.

But it's one thing to enjoy a countryside repose and another to be put out to pasture. What I mean is this: however you choose to define retirement, it should not lead you to grazing on the grass of inactivity. Opportunities to contribute and share your talents, gifts, knowledge, and experience still exist, even at this juncture. Whether or not you avail yourself of those opportunities—that's up to you. Bottom line: being retired should not be the death knell to a life of participation and involvement.

In an article entitled "I'm 78 and Refuse to Retire—Here Are 9 Things About Happiness and Money We're Often Taught Too Late," Peter Buckman calls retirement a "nonsensical term."[8] Self-employed and still engaged at seventy-eight, he says, "To call yourself retired is a totally inaccurate description of all the activities and anxieties that fill your waking—and often your sleeping—hours. Just because you're no longer in full-time employment doesn't mean you have withdrawn from the world, or that you have nothing more to contribute."[9] Simply put, he's saying it's foolish to relinquish an active work life based on age. "Perhaps your philosophy of a work life could [or should] include your own imagination of how your later years should be spent," as Thomas Moore states in *A Life at Work: The Joy of Discovering What You Were Born to Do*.[10]

As you grow older, the circumstances surrounding your career—and life—change. As a result, the extensive responsibilities of your role, for example, may now be too burdensome: you can no longer carry the weight of such a demanding position. Or maybe your interests have evolved and you no longer want to do for a living what you've been doing. You'd prefer to explore other options. It's possible you now have the financial flexibility to turn your "dream job," that thing you've always wanted to do, into reality. You may even want to explore more creative outlets, like art or music, whether they generate an income or not. Or maybe unexpected changes at home—an aging parent perhaps—require you to find a job with a less traditional employment structure, something part-time or a role that allows you to work from home.

Your situation can change for a host of reasons. Numerous events can impact your work world. There's no doubt about this. It wouldn't take much to generate a long list of how one's world can be turned upside down in a blink of an eye. And to boot, the real kicker is that no one can predict when these life- and career-altering events might arrive; life's surprises spring up without warning. Even when we sense some change may be coming around the corner, we never really know the exact moment it will present itself. And crystal ball gazing—that's just a fool's attempt to pull back the curtain hiding those future occurrences.

None of these unexpected events, however, regardless of when they reveal themselves, have to dictate how you choose to define the latter stage of your employment journey. The power to shape that time period still resides—and always will—with you. If nothing else, Buckman's article is a simple reminder and sound admonition not to fall asleep behind the wheel of your career vehicle.

When I was a teenager, I caught a ride to a concert with a buddy of mine. The show was in Asbury Park, a couple hours from where I lived in Rockaway, New Jersey. Regardless, I had to go. For God's sake, I had front row tickets to the Allman Brothers Band!

Driving there was a blast; getting home, not so much.

The ride there was a drug- and alcohol-fueled jaunt, and despite that, there were no issues. (Let the record reflect, I understand how irresponsible and reckless it is to drive under the influence. I acknowledge that.) Luckily, we made it to the show.

We also got lucky on our way home, but to say we didn't tempt fate would be a lie. We partied like rock stars on the way to the concert and did the same during the concert, caring not about being bright-eyed and bushy-tailed—sober—for the ride home. But as everyone knows, the party always ends, and you have to face the music when it does.

A two-hour trek home awaited us. To put it plainly, we were an accident waiting to happen.

We left the task of getting us home safe and sound to the driver, who was just as "toasted" as the rest of us. Asinine. Foolish. Stupid. Idiotic. Mindless. Moronic. Pure insanity. No doubt. Those of us not driving fell asleep instantly.

At a certain point, my friend behind the wheel dozed off, too, and when he did, the car started to veer off the road in the direction of a cliff. If not for a head bob that roused him from his sleepiness, this tale would have ended differently and might be told by someone else. He opened his eyes in the nick of time, steered the wheel away from the road's edge, and averted a heartbreaking disaster—like those you read about in the papers and see on nightly TV broadcasts.

The jerking motion of the car woke everyone up. When we realized what had almost happened, we immediately rolled down the car windows (yes, it was that long ago) to let fresh air fill the vehicle—and our lungs—and then started to chat about the show. A carful of chatterers, we figured, would keep our party-wearied chauffeur from crashing.

This story is by no means an endorsement to use your car as a party bus. To be clear, my friends and I were fools for doing so. If anything, it highlights our ignorance about the dangers of toking and drinking alcohol while driving. That said, I recount the tale here as a warning not to fall asleep behind the wheel of your career vehicle.

Years of work can take a toll on you. "Time," as Michel de Montaigne says, "breaks our strength, and makes us grow feeble."[11] Make no mistake, the hour is late, the road is dark, and the best and strongest among us can nod off.

But when it comes to your career, you need not fall asleep at the wheel. You don't have to plummet down a cliff and meet a sad end. Such falling-asleep-behind-the-wheel career tragedies can be avoided. There are "better safe than sorry" steps and strategies you can take. For now, let's take a moment to think about the "why" of maintaining an active life of employment opposed to retreating into unemployment.

Here are a handful of reasons, listed in no order of importance:

- **It prevents boredom**. Boredom bedevils; boredom besets; boredom burdens. It's the offspring of idleness, and being idle increases misery—misery that could be cured by work. Boredom makes the retired and semiretired pace halls and climb walls. No matter the size of your house, if "retirement" has you spending too much time there, its halls and walls will begin to shrink and close in on you. Doing nothing leads to a lack of wellness. On the other hand, getting out of the house, using your mind and body, and interacting with others at some level fosters and feeds your sense of well-being.

- **It postpones the inevitable**. The day will come when you can't do what you once did or what you'd like to do. The vagaries and frailties of life will make sure of that. That day—when you can no longer do what you want to do or once did—will come whether you like it or not, whether you want it to or not. Make no mistake about it. But by staying busy for as long as you can, you can keep that day at bay a bit longer. It's coming. Why invite it to come sooner than necessary?

- **It keeps cash flow flowing**. Regardless of how your financial picture looks, regardless of the state of your portfolio, regardless of the revenue streams you may have created for your retirement years, and whether or not your financial house is in order, it is best to maintain an inbound stream of cash for as long as you can.

  In his book *The Bell Lap: The 8 Biggest Mistakes to Avoid as You Approach Retirement*, Joseph R. Hearn addresses the reason why when he says, "While we can purchase life insurance to protect our family if we die prematurely, no one has developed longevity insurance to provide for every need if we live for a long, long time."[12] At every stage of your career, maintaining a policy of making money—rather than not making it—is a wise one to follow. Money makes the world go round, and therefore, you'll need it to reach the end of the road. My advice: keep filling the money box as much as possible so you'll have what you need for the kind of future you want to live. To the best of your ability, put off tapping into any funds you have saved for as long as you can to avoid the challenges associated with outliving your money.

- **It promotes a sense of usefulness**. My dad disliked retirement because he hated no longer having a job to check in to. He felt he still had something left to offer. If it were up to him, he would have continued working as long as someone wanted him. During the late 1980s and early 1990s, however, an extensive wave of consolidation hit the banking industry, and the day came when there was no longer a need for a man like my dad—a person who had cultivated skills and experience in one sector alone. Unfortunately, management never considered his transferable skills or found new outlets for him to contribute. In today's work world, the onus is on you to ensure others see that you still have something to offer. For those who meaningfully contribute, there will always be a seat at the table—but you must demonstrate your usefulness. Never allow the currency of your abilities to be devalued.

Getting older does not mean you are destined to live a bored and tired existence for the rest of your days. Getting older does not mean you cannot continue to earn a living. And getting older does not mean you are useless and have nothing left to contribute to an organization. Though you're aging, you need not hasten toward a life of inactivity. You can still find and explore avenues whereby you feel productive and are able to express and share your gifts, talents, knowledge, and passions. Being older doesn't mean you have to call it quits.

2
RESISTANCE IS NOT FUTILE

RECLAIM YOUR INNER REBEL

THERE ARE TWO CHRISTMAS MOVIES I love more than all others. The first is *Rudolph the Red-Nosed Reindeer* because of its reference to the Island of Misfit Toys. Who hasn't, at one time or another, felt like a misfit? Being a square peg in a round hole, a fish out of water, a person who doesn't quite fit in—it's a feeling we've all experienced at least once in our lives. Maybe even in a job.

It's how I felt when I worked for a subsidiary of Deloitte and Touche, where almost all of my coworkers were Big 4 alumni—and I wasn't. My role? Finding jobs for accounting and finance professionals looking to build careers in corporate America. While I never doubted my ability to do the job, one fact made me feel a bit out of place: my educational background was completely different from everyone else's. They had bachelor's or master's degrees in accounting; I was a former minister with a master's in theological studies. In other words, I was the only reindeer with a red nose; I hailed from the Island of Misfit Toys.

The second Christmas movie in my top two is *Santa Claus Is Comin' to Town*. In it, Burgermeister Meisterburger says to a young Kris Kringle, who just started his career of gift giving, "You are obviously a nonconformist and a rebel."

Nonconformity, the conscious choice to take alternative approaches to the mainstream, is a necessary trait if you hope to conclude your career on a high note. To finish strong and cross the tape at the finish line with purpose, you'll need to define retirement on your own terms—not by following the crowd. You must be a nonconformist and a rebel. And to do so, you'll need to reclaim your inner rebel.

If you're lucky, you've never lost your revolutionary self—the spirit you had as a teenager that made you go against everything your parents said and drives you to fight for what's important, for what's "right," at least right for you. Unfortunately, as we age, most of us lose the will to follow this path.

But a fighting spirit is exactly what must be recovered.

The workplace is full of aimless agitators, rudderless renegades, and mad mutineers—those people who revolt against "the system" without any relevant intention. They complain and curse about how their company operates, how it squeezes its staff into a mold, how it dehumanizes employees, and how it stifles individuality. But there's no purpose behind their malcontent. They're rebellious for the sake of rebelliousness. They dislike their situation but do nothing to change it. They prefer only to complain.

That's not the kind of rebellion I'm suggesting.

The workplace is also crowded with people willing to become part of "the collective." For some, joining a Borg-like entity makes sense. What drives that? The need for security? A steady paycheck? Fear of the unknown? Are they risk averse or simply scared to bet on themselves and strike out on their own? Who knows—it could be one of these, a combination, or all of the above.

They're content punching their hours, making sure the "machine" functions as it should. Going through the motions without purpose or meaning makes sense to them, I suppose. Sadly, there's never been, nor will there ever be, a shortage of droid-like employees willing to sacrifice their individuality, calculating that the cost of maintaining their singularity is too high a price to pay.

The typical employee supposes that holding on to one's uniqueness in corporate America's machine-like environment is too hard. Resistance is futile, right? According to them, it's easier to surrender and be absorbed into the entity.

Defying the establishment certainly takes bravery and nerve. Being a beacon of individuality in an Orwellian *1984*-type environment is tough business. But the alternative— being molded and mechanized by such an environment—is a soul-sapping journey downward into an aimless abyss. It'll get you nowhere; it has no destination. As J. Paul Getty says in his essay "The Art of Individuality," "few—if any— people who insist on squeezing themselves into stereotyped molds will ever get very far on the road to success [or in their career]."[1] This should be motivation enough to take up arms.

To be fair, in recent years companies have worked to foster a more diverse workforce and have embraced the varied view-points that come with it. Steps have been taken to humanize the workplace and make it less driven by what Getty calls the "Cult of Conformity." More than ever, companies appreciate individuality and understand the importance of diversity as a means to a stronger workforce. Undoubtedly, we are far from the working world of the Industrial Age.

But let's not kid ourselves: many organizations still prize and push uniformity over individuality. Old habits die hard, as the proverb says.

And it makes sense for employers to do so.

For one, similarity in the workforce removes the complexities that come with a plethora of personas. By forcing employees into a mold—unifying them by making them uniform—companies then need only one approach to "manage" their staff. As I stated in my book *Jump-Start Your Career*, "People are easier to manage when an indistinguishable sameness characterizes them."[2]

Furthermore, this type of approach removes hiring complexities. Recruiting candidates cut from the same cloth simplifies the process: just seek out and hire those with the same educational background, the same pedigree, the same skills, the same style and demeanor, the same mind-set, the same look and feel. This way, you always know what you're getting. Why bother with someone who thinks differently, who thinks outside the box? That's more work, an employer might say.

The main problem with this tactic is that it fails to account for one very significant X factor: people. You just never know when one out of the bunch might rise up, discontented and dissatisfied with how they're being treated or perceiving themselves to be treated.

And when it comes to asserting your individuality, sometimes that's what it takes. You have to upend any rigid rules about employment in the final stage that have taken up residence in the corners of your mind. You have to get mad as hell because, deep down, something feels wrong. In this case, you're feeling the stirrings of late-stage employment, and you believe you still have more to contribute, no matter what the company, society, or the world may say.

Maybe you've started to believe the myth that you have nothing left to offer an organization. Maybe a cloud of ageism has started to blind you to the reality that there's still a role you can play, that you can still be a factor within a company. Maybe your employer has suggested taking a "package" — code for, "Your value has dwindled, so now is the right time for you to pack it in . . . maybe for good."

Or maybe you've started to doubt yourself. The fact is, you are older. Yes, wiser. Yes, more experienced than most. Yes, probably someone who knows more about the company than those offering you a packaged deal. But older nonetheless, and possibly feeling your age. And because of that, you are now questioning your ability to contribute.

If that's the case, then I suggest following the example of Howard Beale, who was feeling his rage in the 1976 movie *Network*. Beale is an anchor for Union Broadcasting System's *UBS Evening News*, and while on air, he goes on a tirade about how bad things have become in the working world and the world at large. He references an economic depression, people losing their jobs, banks going under, crime on the rise, and political turmoil. Sound familiar?

Some question his sanity; he seems unhinged. Others wonder if he's inspired—maybe even an oracle with a message from some transcendent entity. Nevertheless, the end of his rant captures the fighting spirit needed to overcome the flawed corporate myth about age and one's ability to contribute toward the end of one's career.

Here's what he trumpeted for all *UBS Evening News* viewers to hear: "All I know is first you got to get mad. You've got to say: 'I'm mad as hell and I'm not going to take this anymore. I'm a human being, goddammit. My life has value.' So I want you to get up now. I want you to get out of your chairs and go to the window, open it, and stick your head out and yell. I want you to yell: 'I'm mad as hell and I'm not going to take this anymore!'"[3]

Can you relate to Beale's exclamation? Does his vehemence resonate with you? Have your work years drubbed you into thinking you have nothing left to offer but deep down you know it's not true?

If so, it's time to challenge that empty-headed employment myth that says you have nothing more to contribute just because you're older. If so, are you prepared to get up and do something about it? Are you willing to reclaim your inner rebel and rise up against such nonsense?

Sadly, most won't.

Most will continue to go with the flow, accept what the company is telling them, and then drift into retired life. Soon enough, they figure, they'll have the grass of inactivity to graze on, and that should be sufficient sustenance to live off. Those who think in this manner tend to be the same individuals who acquiesce to the company's preference for uniformity— or perhaps have an innate propensity for it.

It's tempting, toward the end of your career, either to meaninglessly be a part of something—what equates to a robotic approach to employment—or to not be employed at all. Christine McVie's idea of quiet repose in England's countryside doesn't sound all that bad. And it wouldn't be—as long as you continued to share your gifts and talents in some meaningful way.

That's why this phase, like every other phase in one's employment journey, requires a rebellious spirit—a respectfully resistant attitude against traditional thinking that seeks to push you in a not-so-gentle manner into that good night of retirement. A better option—and one this book espouses—is to locate your inner resister and repudiate any old logic that uses age as a barometer for whether or not you have something left to contribute.

According to Francesca Gino, author of *Rebel Talent: Why it Pays to Break the Rules at Work and in Life*, you might actually be surprised at how this makes you feel. "What my research suggests is that we can actually bring more joy into our lives by being rebels: by behaving in ways that defy conformity."[4]

If breaking the rules comes with surprising benefits, what then can we do to combat our tendency to trace patterns already established? What can we do at this juncture in our career to be less orthodox, less stereotypical, less customary? How do we let people know we are "mad as hell" and not going to take it anymore? In other words, when we rebel, how should we do it, and what should we rebel against?

After thirty-plus years of providing career guidance to professionals, I believe there are at least three ways to rebel—to rage against the machine, so to speak—and there are four attitudes you should defy at this stage in your career.

THREE WAYS TO REBEL

1. Mindfully—Embrace a "Not Giving a F*ck" Mind-set
Take a cue from Mark Manson's *The Subtle Art of Not Giving a F*ck: A Counterintuitive Approach to Living a Good*

Life. His philosophy encourages focusing only on what truly matters and discarding everything else. As Manson puts it, "Maturity is what happens when one learns to only give a fuck about what's truly fuckworthy."[5] This mind-set helps put life and career decisions in the right perspective.

Manson's point isn't about indifference; it's about prioritization. In the context of your career, it's about focusing less on others' opinions and more on how you choose to spend your time. Ultimately, it's your journey, and you have every right to make decisions that align with your goals and values.

Does this sound rebellious? Absolutely. And if anyone's earned a right to be a little defiant, it's someone who has been through the ups and downs of career development—and life. Age brings privilege, and one of those privileges is knowing when to tell others to step aside—or in less polite terms, to f*ck off. And trust me, it feels good. It's a satisfying kind of "senior moment."

2. Respectfully—Defy but Maintain Deference

Defiance doesn't have to be a zero-sum game. You can rebel while respecting others and leaving room for mutual benefit. How you choose to push back is just as important as the rebellion itself.

My business partner and I once faced a management team that saw us as relics, no longer fit to lead. Their "vision" did not align with our approach, even though it had generated a 42 percent gross margin, nor with their business model for the future. But due to the terms of our employment contracts, removing us would come at a high cost to the company.

When we met to discuss their plan, they offered a payout far below what we were contractually owed. Our response was clear: "No way." We knew our value, and we resisted their lowball offer. However, our defiance was paired with enough respect to keep the conversation open. We ultimately reached an agreement that benefitted both sides.

The takeaway? You can stand your ground while keeping things civil. A respectful approach to rebellion often leads to win-win situations.

As you navigate the latter stages of your career, you don't need to bulldoze others. There's power in defying expectations while still showing respect. When you rise up, do so with dignity.

3. Wholeheartedly—Commit Fully

When it comes to rebellion, half measures won't work; you must be resolute. To resist effectively, unwavering commitment is essential. Embrace your cause fully, stand firm, and give it your all. Double-minded people are like kites in the wind, blown this way and that. This resolve is crucial because resistance to your actions is almost inevitable.

Consider the lives of Mahatma Gandhi, Jesus, Nelson Mandela, Malala Yousafzai, Mother Teresa, and Martin Luther King Jr., to name a few. Each was viewed as a rebel for one reason or another. By standing up for what they believed to be right, they all faced fierce resistance. Those who rebel against inaccurate employment myths are sure to face opposition. So when you rebel against an erroneous career myth, be prepared to do it without reservation.

WHAT TO REBEL AGAINST

Once you understand *how* to rebel, it's crucial to know *what* to rebel against. Here are four unhelpful attitudes you should resist:

1. The Old Ways of Doing Things

Stop clinging to what worked in the past and start focusing on what will drive future success. The strategies that got you here won't necessarily take you to the next level. Break away from outdated playbooks, and create a new one that suits where you want to go.

Think outside the box, take advice selectively, and make decisions that reflect who you are now. Remember, you don't have to be the same person you were in your twenties, thirties, or even forties. Reinvention is key.

2. The Tendency to Waste Time

Most of us think we have more time than we do, and all of us waste more of it than we should. But at this stage in your career, time is too precious to squander. This doesn't mean you need to be in a rush, though. There's wisdom in pacing yourself while staying focused on what truly matters.

My wife often reminds me, "Not everything has to be the Amazing Race." She's right. The goal isn't to rush to the finish line. Instead, it's about constantly defining and redefining what that finish line means to you. "You define the finish line," says Phil Knight in *Shoe Dog: A Memoir by the Creator of Nike*.[6] So push that finish line into the future for as long as you can. What's essential is to keep moving forward at a pace that makes sense for you.

3. The Misconception That Old Dogs Can't Learn New Tricks

The adage that old dogs can't learn new tricks is snappy but untrue. Older dogs—and people—have the capacity to learn well into their senior years.

Here's what a couple of veterinarians say in an article entitled "Can Old Dogs Learn New Tricks?": "Even though young pups may be more actively curious, dogs never stop learning. In fact, adult dogs are often easier to train than their younger canine friends specifically because they are not as active. Older dogs are not as easily distracted as pups and can focus for longer periods of time. This ability to concentrate helps them learn new routines more easily."[7]

Just as older dogs can focus better and learn routines more easily than younger pups, seasoned professionals have their own advantages too. They are better equipped to translate experience into an actionable strategy and decipher what's truly important versus what's inconsequential, for example. Your experience and ability to concentrate can help you keep up with evolving workplace trends. You're still capable of learning new tricks, adapting to change, and staying relevant—assuming you remain willing to grow.

So as the workplace identifies new and more advanced ways of doing "the job," and as technologies continue to develop at warp speed, and as the world and the working world continue to evolve, you can learn along with everyone else. There's no need to be kept in the dark of "old school" ways of thinking.

4. Thinking in Terms of Better or Worse

Don't fall into the trap of thinking that younger and middle-aged years are better and more productive and older years are less so. Instead, view your career as a series of distinct periods, privileged intervals of time between successive occurrences, each with its own value.

Art aficionados and historians by and large divide Pablo Picasso's career into ten periods characterized by particular styles and themes:

- The Blue Period (1901–1904): distinguished by blue tones and themes of poverty and suffering. Was this his "starving artist" stage?
- The Rose Period (1904–1906): marked by warmer colors and circus-related works. Probably a fun and happy stage. Maybe a whimsical, "clowning around" phase?
- The Primitivism Period (1907–1909): influenced by African and Iberian art, which led to Cubism. Being truly influenced requires being open to new ideas.
- The Analytic Cubism Period (1909–1912): noted for his use of fragmented form. Sometimes we reach a point where everything feels disjointed, not completely put together.
- The Synthetic Cubism Period (1912–1919): when he integrated collage and other materials into his works. There may be periods of disjointedness, but then we start to put the pieces together.
- The Classical Period (1920s): showcased his return to classical styles. A return to what is traditional, maybe even basic or rudimentary, can be a good thing.
- The Neoclassical Period (1920s–1930s): represented a more traditional and classical approach. Who doesn't appreciate the classics?

- The Surrealist Period (1930s): highlighted surrealist, dreamlike, and fantastical elements. At times, we all wish the world were different. To live a life of illusion can be appealing. The older I get, the more I dream and wish.
- The Post-War Period (1945–1960): incorporated various styles, including a return to figurative and classical forms. As time goes by, we see the benefit of a number of approaches and styles.
- The Later Period (1960s–1973): combined a mix of styles and experimentation. Somehow, as we age, we become more able to draw from all our experiences and blend them into something beautiful.

The seasonality of Picasso's work life reflected the changes he underwent—in both thought and approach—and how those shifts influenced the way he portrayed himself to the world through the medium of art.

Whose career hasn't been marked by a blue (melancholic) period or a "rosy" (flourishing) one? Whose path hasn't been shaped by the thoughts and approaches of others? Who hasn't felt their career to be somewhat fragmented, like broken pieces without cohesion? Who hasn't tried to integrate bits of what they've learned from one job into the next to help shape who they are or aspire to be as an employee? Who hasn't revisited the basics a time or two, reminding themselves of the traits—like hard work and the willingness to start from the bottom—that got them where they are? And surely, some have, in an effort to "forget about life for a while," ventured off on tangents to explore the surreal and fantastical. Ultimately, each career phase we experience leads to a "later period," where we might blend together every piece and fragment of our professional journey, experimenting with the totality of what we've gathered over the years.

Notable careers are made up of pieces from various phases. No single period is better than the other; each has its own merits and contributes to a rich, cumulative tapestry. How that tapestry is woven depends on the person at the loom, so to speak. "No one is the same at forty and at seventy [or at any period of time], but the changes can compose a story that rings true. . . .We compose our lives in time, improvising and responding to context, yet *weaving* threads of continuity and connecting the whole as we move back and forth in memory" (italics mine).[8]

You can choose to rebel against thinking in terms of better or worse and instead embrace the intervals of your career holistically, as a beautiful fabric that reflects every season of your professional journey woven over time.

Rebellion for its own sake is foolish. But rebelling with a purpose—especially against the myths and misconceptions about aging—is powerful. As you navigate the latter stages of your career and rebel for the right reason(s) . . . now that's a different thing altogether. When it comes to this period, resist the idea that age limits your ability to contribute. You still have value, insight, and plenty of fight left.

So go ahead—embrace the rebel within and defy the limiting beliefs that don't serve you.

3
AN APPRECIATION OF VARIATION

REMEMBER AND REPRISE.

RECLAIMING YOUR INNER REVOLUTIONARY SPIRIT is difficult if you have no sense of self. It necessitates knowing yourself and what you believe is worth fighting for. So it bears repeating and reminding: be true to yourself because the best careers are had by those who explore employment channels that allow their individuality to shine.

Raised by a father who worked as a local wine broker and refereed rugby matches, it's no surprise that those same interests threaded their way into the heart and soul of Gérard Bertrand. Born and raised in the heart of Languedoc, France—a 150-mile stretch of land along the Mediterranean coast—Bertrand spent summers working in vineyards and eventually became a professional rugby player. At six feet five inches, he was a formidable opponent, and at that size, he stood out: everyone knew who he was.

That fame, he thought, might come in handy once he started his career in winemaking. He quickly learned, however, that name recognition alone was not enough to open doors in the business. The initial wines he produced were not that good, and the history of wine production in that region didn't help either—their reputation was as rotten as grape black rot. Gérard understood that his first order of business was to address issues of quality.

So he undertook what he called a "quality revolution."[1] The desire to put forth a quality work product came naturally to Gérard. It was part of his DNA. His father had originally promoted the improvement of wine quality in Languedoc by introducing more modern winemaking techniques.

People who know Gérard Bertrand are aware of his uniqueness. Kristen Bieler, in her *Wine Spectator* article titled "His Place in the Sun," says he has "the restlessness of a man on a mission" and that "there is something almost un-French about his boundless ambition." Longtime winemaker Jean-Claude Berrouet said that while Gérard is very much his father's son, sharing his dad's two passions of winemaking and rugby, he still "found his own route to fulfillment and self-expression."[2]

Men and women "on a mission" are some of the most divergent, "I've got to be me" people you will meet. They know themselves all too well and are so committed to whatever it is they feel called to do that they find it impossible to take their cues from others. They feel compelled to follow their hearts and find their own "route to fulfillment and self-expression."

When Bertrand speaks about making wines, for example, he sounds spiritual. It's one of the things that makes him, well, him. He speaks about opening one's heart to the land to hear what it is saying. He talks about connecting with the surrounding environment and listening to the magic of a vineyard, the vibe it gives when you walk through it. This mentality also extends to how he farms: "For Bertrand, the technical results are less important than the emotional dimension created through [a] sacred method of farming."[3]

Maybe that's why he says his dream only becomes a reality "when people can taste the soul of [the] terroir."[4]

Such language is more religious than secular. "Opening your heart," "listening to the magic," "emotional dimensions created through [a] sacred method," and "taste the soul"—this is the language of Sunday morning church services.

For all of Bertrand's success in the business of wine-making—wine produced from seventeen estates and 2,200 vineyard acres, the purchase of Henri de Toulouse-Lautrec's former Château de Céleyran, his eventual expansion in the American market, and more—he still knows what makes him tick and what makes him feel most himself. His daughter Emma put it best: "People see him as a businessman, but they don't understand he is in the vineyards all the time—that is where he is really himself."[5]

And at fifty-nine, he still has his hands on the wheel of his career vehicle and is not in danger of falling asleep at it. As Bieler says at the end of her article, "Bertrand is still very much in forward motion; age has done little to slow him down."[6]

Bertrand, like seventy-eight-year-old Peter Buckman, has retired the idea of retirement. There's no way he will remove himself to some French countryside and graze on the grass of inactivity. He's committed to being true to himself and to continuing to explore the various avenues winemaking affords and, in doing so, maintain an active life.

Similarly, no one ever accused Dennis Charles Pratt of not being himself. Better known as Quentin Crisp, he was an openly gay English writer, entrepreneur, and actor who intentionally defied societal expectations. Like Gérard Bertrand, he too stood out, though not because of his size.

Crisp took at face value Oscar Wilde's words, "Be yourself; everyone else is taken," and gained fame in England for being unapologetically flamboyant. Eventually, he crossed the pond and brought that same panache to the United States.

From 1970 to 1980, he produced a one-man show called "An Evening with Quentin Crisp" and in 1975 wrote a book called *How to Have a Lifestyle*. Both afforded him a platform to discuss his unique life experiences and observations with the signature flair and flamboyance for which he became known.

At the time, British and American societies were not as "evolved" as they are today; Crisp faced suppressive discrimination and crushing prejudice. Yet he remained true to himself and continued to promote uniqueness with wit and a singularity of style. Stars can't help but shine brightly against dark backgrounds.

People who are doggedly determined to be true to themselves encourage it in others, including, and maybe especially, the "strange," the "unusual," the "unorthodox," and the "misfit." Someone who appreciates and respects his or her individuality wants you to be uniquely you too. "In the end," Crisp encourages, "you have only one thing to offer the world that no one else can give, and that is yourself."[7]

Most everyone has seen the now-infamous shower scene in the movie *Jerry Maguire* when Jerry, played by Tom Cruise, says, "Help me, help you," to Rod Tidwell, played by Cuba Gooding Jr. If you haven't, it's a must-see.

As often happens to agents representing sports professionals, Jerry is dealing with a couple of negotiation challenges related to Rod's contract: Rod doesn't quite fit the bill of the stereotypical wide receiver because he's too small, and he also comes to the table with an attitude. Because of that, the team hoping to recruit him expects a discount on his price tag.

Jerry needs Rod's help to overcome the objections of his client and says to Rod, "We want more from them, so let's give them more; let's show them your pure joy of the game. Let's bury the attitude a little bit and show them—"

Rod, taken aback, interrupts Jerry and says, "Wait! You're telling me to dance." He thinks what Jerry is really asking him to do is to conform to how others promote themselves, and he just isn't willing to sacrifice his individuality in an effort to achieve marketing success.

Jerry clarifies his own intentions and says, "No. I'm saying let's get back to the guy who first started playing the game. *Remember* . . . way back when you were a kid" (italics mine).[8]

Many travelers on their career journey forget who they are, that person deep down at the core of their being. Somewhere along the way, they lose themselves. "People change in the maze," says Dumbledore to those competing for the Triwizard Cup in the movie *Harry Potter and the Goblet of Fire*. He then reminds the competitors to take care because "you could just lose yourself along the way."[9] And losing yourself, whether in your career or life, is the worst possible thing that can happen. To avoid that, one must reflect and reconnect with his or her true self, like Bertrand and Crisp, who thoroughly knew themselves and were thereby able to explore directions that gave full expression to their personas.

By remembering—or rediscovering—your true self, I do not mean to imply that you must become exactly the same person you were earlier in your career or life. Your tastes, values, preferences, and interests change over time. Surely, you're a more mature and evolved professional compared to when you first embarked on your career journey. It's impossible to be the same person you were so many years ago. "It's no use going back to yesterday, because I was a different person then,"[10] says Alice in Lewis Carroll's *Alice in Wonderland.*

But a "life review—remembering who [you] have been—offers a way of mining the past for the strengths needed in the present."[11] In other words, taking time to remember who you were over the years helps with reprising yourself for the here and now and beyond. Let me explain.

In music, a reprise refers to a version of a song that is similar to, yet different from, the song on which it is based. Sections of songs heard earlier in a composition, album, or live performance are repeated. Think of how the theme song for a James Bond movie gets woven throughout the entire film. Over and over, at different stages and in different scenes, the motif or signature tune subtly rests in the background, but with tweaks and variations.

As you move through the stages of your career—the musical scores of your career, so to speak—and especially as you contemplate how to stay active through its latter phase, you must reprise the song of who you are. How can you modify the song for this stage of your career journey? It's not possible to be the same employee you were years ago, but you can be a new version of yourself without sacrificing the person you've always been. You can nod to your history while embracing a new and different future. Reprising allows you to recall and reference the person you've been at your core while still planning for the future you want to create.

By creating variations and considering alternatives to the single theme of who you are—by re-composing your essence—the lifespan of your career becomes a living work of art, an iterative process.

My own career remains a work in progress. Maybe it offers some hints as to what I mean by all this.

Earlier in my career, I decided to become a minister, a unique career for sure. My motivation behind this decision, aside from feeling called to do it, was a desire to help people on their spiritual journeys. And being a pastor afforded me the opportunity to do just that.

To prepare for such an endeavor, I studied theology for nine years—one should never enter the ministry willy-nilly, I figured. Coupled with this were hours spent assisting churches by leading Bible studies and worship, serving as a youth minister, and organizing outreach services. Ultimately, I became a full-fledged pastor and shepherded a small flock.

My life as a minister, however, did not work out as I had planned, and for personal reasons, I resigned from that post.

During that time, I supplemented my income by working part-time at a bank. (Not all ministry jobs pay well.) My dad had been a banker his entire adult life, and he found me a job through one of his connections. That didn't mean, however, that I wanted to be a banker too. Still, after resigning from the ministry, it was nice to have a job while I tried to figure out what was next for me.

Little did I know that I would have to figure things out sooner rather than later. Unexpectedly, the division at the bank where I worked was sold to another bank based in Minnesota; my job was still mine if I wanted it, but it would be located there—not in sunny Southern California. Those of us in that division had a year to decide, a luxury of time that you wouldn't be afforded in today's working world.

After the announcement, I wasted no time and went directly to my office to start looking for a new job. An ad in the paper caught my attention: "Seeking Managers—Call the Number Below." Since I was a manager, I figured I was qualified. In my naiveté, it seemed that simple. So I called.

In short order, I was scheduled for an interview with Robert Half International, at the time the world's largest staffing firm. For reasons that became clear later, the person I met with focused not on my management experience at the bank but rather on my preparation for the ministry and my pastoral duties.

"Having a message seems important to you," she said. "Why don't you make the service offerings of Robert Half your new message?"

The job required speaking to potential clients about their staffing needs, presenting RHI's capabilities in meeting those needs, and developing relationships with clients and potential candidates we would send out on assignment. What was clear to her (and not to me until later) was that there was an overlap between the skills I had cultivated for the ministry and the skills required for this job. Her comment about having a message resonated with me, so I accepted her offer to work there.

As time went by, I grew to appreciate the thread that wove itself through my work as a minister and my work in the staffing world. In the former, I provided spiritual guidance; in the latter, career guidance. Both allowed me to help people during different phases of their lives.

Thirty-plus years later, I am still finding employment opportunities for people. Now I am also writing books on career development in an attempt to help people, in some small way, as they navigate their career journeys.

Different platforms—the ministry, the staffing industry, and book writing—have allowed me to splinter off from the core theme of my life's work, which is helping others. And in the process, I've been creating my own career composition.

Let's say you feel your career is a hodgepodge of disparate parts—roles you took on that have no clear rhyme or reason. Let's say none of what you have done to date shows any real connection to a theme. Let's say your career path has been littered with steps and missteps that show no clear direction. That's okay. Career compositions—and life compositions—are made from the materials you have on hand. Careers and lives are Frankenstein-like, built from parts stitched together to create something greater—and stronger—than the individual parts themselves.

Think about it like this: careers consist of numerous components, making them more complex than you may think. *Webster's New Universal Unabridged Dictionary* defines *complex* in a nuanced fashion, noting its Latin derivation from a word that means "to weave and to braid." Complex constructs are composed of interlaced strands that form a more intricate pattern, like a stylish hair braid or boat rope. Likewise, all careers are woven together, made from strands found and formed over the course of one's employment history.

And it's never too late, so don't even go there about not having enough time, even at this stage, to build a career. Past career moves need not limit or constrain the infinite possibilities of the future. Remember that whatever was cultivated at each stage of your career can be carried over into each subsequent stage. As diverse and divergent as each stage may be, they all contribute to your overall employment "body of work."

There is one exception to my rule of reprise, however, and that is when you've determined that a total, full-blown, full-scale, complete, thorough, overall, unconditional, full-fledged reinvention of yourself is in order—you can no longer be who you were, nor do you want to do anything remotely close to what you've been doing. You've decided, like a snake, to shed your skin to allow for continued growth. You must do something entirely different because "the expected value of your path is [no longer] the same as when you initially chose it," as Annie Duke says in her book *Quit: The Power of Knowing When to Walk Away*.[12] (It should be noted that Duke left a life in academia to become a professional gambler—a radical redefinition of her career plans for sure).

Ultimately, whether you choose to reprise the overarching theme of your career or decide to reinvent yourself completely, the key is to remain intentional and authentic in your journey. Careers, like life itself, are not always linear—they twist, turn, and sometimes take unexpected detours. But whether you're refining a familiar path or forging a brand-new one, embracing the changes with purpose and conviction allows you to stay true to who you are—or who you're becoming. After all, your career is your story to tell, your song to sing, and how you compose it is entirely up to you.

4

CHANGING LANES

REDEFINE YOUR CAREER.

CHOOSING REINVENTION OVER A REPRISE doesn't necessarily imply dissatisfaction with your career or the person you've become. Rather, it may reflect a readiness for a profound transformation, fueled by a desire to go far beyond the familiar boundaries of a reprise. It's not always about splintering off from the overarching theme of your career; it can also be about embracing something wholly different—a reinvention and redefinition. Sometimes the urge to head in a completely new direction means you need to switch lanes to reach where you truly want to be.

In jam sessions, jazz musicians do this sort of thing all the time. They often deviate from prior notes, preceding riffs, and previously struck chords because they're seeking out the unplayed, unstrummed, and unexpressed melodies within them—music that needs a new avenue for expression. Similarly, there are moments—especially in the later stages of your career—when you, too, feel the need to strike a different chord, and all you require is a fresh channel through which to bring that new expression to life.

One artist who has definitively struck his own chord in the process of reinventing himself is Calvin Broadus Jr., affectionately known to his fans as Snoop Dogg. At fifty-two years old, the D-O-double-G has figured out ways to keep rocking and rolling and rapping—and then some—down the road. (Snoop actually serves as an example of someone who has both reprised and reinvented himself; he has maintained his music career but has diversified into completely different ventures.)

Since his Death Row Records days, a period that included stints in and out of prison and being a key figure in the establishment of West Coast rap, he's been busy exploring other avenues. Most recently, he served as torchbearer at the Paris Olympics, earning him the title of "peace messenger," a moniker afforded all Olympic torchbearers. But even this pales in comparison to his numerous advertising contracts—a list of no fewer than thirteen—and includes companies like Petco, Corona, Cadbury, Michelin Tires, General Insurance, Hot Pockets, T-Mobile, and Tostitos.

Along with commercials, Snoop has also had small roles in movies and has explored business opportunities that include a licensing deal to bring a red wine to market, a joint venture with Happi Foodi, a cannabis brand, and a start-up called Gin and Juice. On top of this, he'll be spinning out a new album called *Missionary*.

Snoop gets at the secret behind his apparent success when he tells Matt Craig in his article "Snoop Dreams," "What I didn't do was try to follow the fads or the trends. I just stayed me the whole way."[1]

Many other well-known figures have embraced reinvention. After years as a boxer, George Foreman transformed himself into an entrepreneur, preacher, chef, and TV personality, achieving major success with his iconic George Foreman Grill. Martha Stewart began her career as a stockbroker before reinventing herself as a successful caterer, ultimately building an empire in media, publishing, and home decor. Arnold

Schwarzenegger evolved from a champion bodybuilder to a Hollywood action star, and later into a politician, serving as governor of California. Vera Wang started as a figure skater and then worked as a fashion editor before shifting careers in her forties to become a leading bridal and fashion designer.

My favorite example of career reinvention—or reimagining what your work life can become, even later in life—is Colonel Harland David Sanders, the founder of Kentucky Fried Chicken. His journey to becoming a fast-food icon demonstrates that anyone can transform and redefine their career, regardless of age.

Growing up without a father, Harland assumed many responsibilities at a young age, including cooking for his family—a task that likely ignited his interest in food. Over the years, he worked various jobs, from farmhand to streetcar conductor, to insurance salesman, and even soldier. His career path was far from linear.

Eventually, Colonel Sanders took over a service station in Corbin, Kentucky, where he began serving meals to travelers in the station's adjoining living area. His fried chicken, made with a secret blend of eleven herbs and spices, quickly gained popularity. His culinary skills earned him the title of Kentucky Colonel, a symbolic honor bestowed by the state's governor. Over the next decade, he perfected his recipe, including a unique pressure-frying method that preserved the chicken's flavor.

However, his restaurant business took a hit when a new interstate highway bypassed his location. So at sixty-five years old, with limited savings and only a modest Social Security check, he decided to franchise his chicken recipe. And then he hit the road.

Sanders pitched his chicken concept to restaurant owners across the United States, offering his recipe in exchange for a small fee for each chicken sold. By the time he was seventy-three, over six hundred KFC outlets were established across the United States and Canada. He eventually sold his corporation for $2 million (equivalent to about $20 million today), becoming a global icon with his image central to KFC's branding worldwide.

While this story is remarkable, it's important to remember that Colonel Sanders wasn't an overnight success at sixty-five, nor was he a household name at that time. Not everyone who successfully reinvents their career becomes famous—but the potential for transformation is universal.

Troy Hill graduated from the University of Oregon with a degree in journalism. Afterward, he landed a job at KZAM, an independently owned radio station he had admired since childhood. Though the work was challenging, it provided him with a deep understanding of the industry and served as a stepping-stone to a successful career in sales. Over time, Troy became adept at making cold calls and building strong relationships, finding satisfaction in his work.

But things changed when a new ownership team took over and altered the way the business operated. Troy sensed that something was off. His passion for the job waned, and he knew it was time to move on.

A few months later, Troy accepted an opportunity with KVAL, a CBS affiliate, where he further honed his skills under an excellent management team. Eventually, he transitioned to a larger market, partly to support his husband's career, and continued his work as a salesperson for KOMO, an ABC affiliate. Over the next twenty-five years, he climbed the corporate ladder, progressing from Account Executive to Regional Account Executive, then to Business Development Manager, and finally to Local Sales Manager. Objectively, he had built an impressive career.

As his career evolved, Troy realized for work to have meaning, he needed to enjoy the people he worked with and had to have a passion for what he did. For those reasons, he focused on working with smaller, locally owned companies. In an email discussion with Troy, he said it allowed him to "tell a story about advertising dollars staying local and supporting the community, not going to New York, or Chicago, or wherever the big corporate offices were."[2]

Eventually, KOMO was sold to Sinclair Broadcasting, a large, publicly traded media company. Once again, Troy felt his passion draining away. At fifty-three, he made the bold decision to give a ninety-day notice, "trusting a new door would open."

A few years later, Troy and his husband moved to a small town in Oregon, partly to be closer to his aging parents. After settling into their new home, he noticed that the house "was yearning for a garden." So, he got to work, transforming a basic, unremarkable yard into a vibrant flower oasis—a process that took about two years. And people noticed!

It wasn't long before a real estate agent asked him to redesign their office landscape. As word spread, people began stopping by, asking for his business card. He soon had to get some printed.

In the meantime, Troy also took on a part-time role with a locally owned community radio station, assisting with fundraising. This work reignited his passion and served as a fitting "last hurrah" for his sales career. Simultaneously, his gardening business flourished. Now, at sixty, he has thirty clients, handling projects both large and small.

Troy reflects on how his life and career have been influenced by a concept from Frank O'Connor's book *An Only Child*. O'Connor recounts how, as a boy, he and his friends would venture across the Irish countryside, often encountering stone walls protecting orchards and livestock. Undeterred, they would throw their wool caps over even the tallest walls and then figure out how to retrieve them.

If asked, Troy would tell you that his career—and life—are the result of throwing his hat over a wall and then finding a way to retrieve it. Not only is he still tossing his hat over walls at sixty, but he's also building them as he provides landscaping services to those in his small community.

Similarly, Paul Verano's career path took an unexpected turn, leading him to redefine his professional life. After graduating with a degree in theater, he initially pursued a career in acting and lighting design. He secured a position with one of Seattle's largest theater companies, focusing on lighting design, and also volunteered in his spare time. This volunteer work eventually opened the door to a career in HIV/AIDS research at the University of Washington and the Fred Hutchinson Cancer Research Center (FHCRC). Over time, lighting design became a side project as Paul transitioned to a full-time role at UW/FHCRC, where he excelled as a recruitment and education coordinator. His innovative recruitment strategies were so effective that they were adopted globally.

Over time, his job became "more and more predictable and tiresome." Paul felt the need for a change. Seeking a fresh start, he moved to New Zealand with his husband, hoping to rejuvenate himself and consider new career possibilities.

During his time in the United States, he had developed a passion for chocolate and baking, frequently creating cakes and desserts for friends' events. He saw potential in pursuing this interest further.

In New Zealand, what began as a baking hobby soon blossomed into something much more significant. Paul's cheesecakes became an instant hit, quickly gaining popularity at parties where they stood out as a unique offering. Word spread, and soon friends and their colleagues began placing orders. Before long, Paul found himself baking through the night in a friend's café after it closed at three p.m., delivering his sought-after desserts by day. The business grew so rapidly that his husband eventually left his job to help Paul expand this thriving cheesecake operation.

Eventually, Paul and his husband returned to Seattle with plans to open a shop dedicated to selling his cheesecakes. They were advised to consider a 490-square-foot space available in Pike Place Market, a highly coveted location. After navigating the rigorous application process, Paul successfully secured the space and opened The Confectional, a bakery specializing in cheesecakes and chocolate truffles, each crafted in a variety of unique flavors.

Following years of success, Paul and his husband decided to step back from the day-to-day operations. They arranged for a business partner to take over the management of The Confectional. Paul personally trained the new manager for a year and remained on call to provide additional support whenever needed, ensuring the continued success of the bakery.

Nowadays, Paul stays active by doing graphic design work for local businesses and creating custom-made T-shirts, which he sells online. He also keeps busy crafting and selling

Glitzmas tree and menorah artwork made from vintage jewelry and lights. On top of that, he makes "big heads" made from papier-mâché for his town's Big Head Parade and works on call at an Italian delicatessen filling in wherever they need him.

What lessons can be drawn from the approaches of Colonel Sanders, Troy Hill, and Paul Verano? The following points are worth considering:

1. **Embrace change willingly**. Be prepared to let go of your established identity. Sanders, Hill, and Verano, as well as Foreman, Stewart, Schwarzenegger, and Wang, stepped out of their comfort zone and ventured into unfamiliar territory. While change can be uncomfortable, it is essential for personal reinvention and growth.

2. **Admit when your current role no longer fulfills you.** Troy Hill was laser-focused on what provided satisfaction in a job: enjoying the people he worked with and having a passion for what he did. When those things disappeared, he left the company he worked for and began to search for something new. Likewise, in an email discussion with Paul Verano, he mentioned his job had grown "more and more predictable and [stale]." It no longer offered a sense of meaning and purpose, and that recognition triggered a need for change. For both Troy and Paul, reinventing themselves allowed them to course-correct career wise.

3. **Remember the importance of patience**. Colonel Sanders spent over a decade perfecting his recipe

before franchising it, and then traveled across the country pitching it to restaurant owners. Similarly, Troy Hill's landscaping business didn't achieve instant success. It started with a personal passion for transforming his own garden. Paul Verano's cheesecake venture started as a hobby also. When others noticed his work, he recognized an opportunity and gradually turned it into a business. Growth was slow but steady.

4. **You call the shots**. Pursue what drives and inspires you and allows you to thrive. Segue into whatever has been calling your name—landscaping, teaching, consulting, philanthropy, counseling, being an executive coach or fitness instructor—the options are limitless. Choose something you've always wanted to do and go for it. What truly matters is staying true to your vision and the reasons behind it.

5. **Honor your passion**. When your work aligns with your passion, it feels less burdensome and more like a meaningful part of your life, leading to increased job satisfaction and overall happiness. Pursuing what you love makes work feel less like a chore and more like a relevant endeavor. Passion naturally fuels motivation, energizing you to accomplish tasks enthusiastically. It puts a "tiger in your tank," as Exxon Mobil's slogan suggests, driving you forward. It also makes you more resilient to challenges, making setbacks and disappointments easier to shrug off.

6. **Adopt unconventionality**. Go against the grain and break away from the norm. Take a step that surprises others—something they'd never expect from you. As

Moore notes in *A Life at Work*, "Today people think that they should be reasonable and conventional in their approach to a career and proceed according to judgments from outside rather than urges from inside."[3] Something very powerful happens when you dare to listen to and follow the unorthodox inclinations of your heart.

While reinventing yourself and your career affords you the opportunity to play to your strengths, follow your interests, and listen to your heart, it may demand more from you. Just because you want to change and take up a very different job or way of life does not mean an easy road lies ahead. However, there are steps you can take to be better prepared.

Starting a new life and shifting into a new direction—whether entering an unfamiliar industry or taking on a new trade—often requires learning new skills and acquiring specialized knowledge. Before embarking on this journey, consider performing a skills gap analysis, then pursue courses, certifications, or hands-on experience to meet the demands of the transition.

To successfully remodel yourself, it's also crucial to assess your financial stability. Consider the financial ramifications of taking such a step, especially if a move like this involves a reduction in your annual income. Planning ahead and eliminating financial surprises is key. As Aesop wisely noted in his *Fables*, "Count the cost before you commit yourself."

If you hope to gain financial benefits (i.e., earn a living) from your new direction, first conduct a study of the market demand for your proposed service or product. Research industry trends to ensure your reinvention is both sustainable and relevant.

Additionally, you should be prepared to check your ego at the door. Becoming the new you and embracing a new role might mean stepping away from leadership positions and learning from others. To use a *Star Wars* analogy, you may shift from being a Jedi—a skilled guardian of peace with the mystical power of the Force, maintaining balance in the galaxy—to a Padawan—an apprentice who needs to learn how to harness the Force and develop light-saber combat skills.

Reinventing yourself requires shifting your mind-set from thinking in terms of "should" to "could."[4] It's about conceptualizing a larger road map and being open to exploring new roads contained within it. It involves breaking free from familiar, ritualistic routines and venturing into uncharted territory. To truly embrace your reinvented self, you must steer your career vehicle beyond the predictable paths and be willing to drive unfamiliar routes. You must be willing to cruise into uncertainty, or as Wes "Scoop" Nisker says, be "hot on the trail of transformation."[5]

The real challenge in leaving behind your old self for a reinvented one lies in the uncertainty of whether the change will be worth it. Unless you're omniscient, there's no way to know if things will unfold as you envision or hope. And that uncertainty can be daunting. As Karen Armstrong reflects in her recounting of the story of Buddha—a prince who abandoned a life of ease and abundance in his father's palace (his comfort zone) to seek a completely different life—"It's frightening to leave our old selves behind, because they are the only way we know how to live. Even if the familiar is unsatisfactory, we tend to cling to it because we are afraid of the unknown."[6]

Yet we would do well to remember the flip side can be just as scary. What if you stay where you are? Your situation remains unchanged, and so do you. Perhaps the scariest thing of all is this: you've stopped growing. Ultimately, you must decide if losing your life to find it is worth it.

5
STROLL DOWN, DON'T PARK ON MEMORY LANE

REMINISCE AND MOVE ON

REMINISCING IS LIKE A SLOW-COOKED stew. The longer past events simmer in the crock pot of your memory, the more their aroma wafts through your mind's kitchen. The same holds true for your career. The more the experiences of your career simmer, the more softly and subtly they permeate your thoughts.

Ideally, the ingredients you've added to the pot—thoughts about the person you were, the person you've become, and the career you've built—are recalled with pleasure. If not, no matter. Most good recipes have a dash of this and a dash of that. Careers are similar; they consist of all sorts of components—right moves and wrong moves, good steps and missteps—all of which contribute to the dish, so to speak.

As previously mentioned, the opportunities that lie ahead are not dictated by your past; your future is shaped by the decisions you make today. Memory lane is only meant for a stroll, not for parking. You shouldn't linger there too long anyway; we don't do well to dwell on yesterday when today and tomorrow are calling for our attention.

That said, when you look back, what kinds of memories are worth recollecting and stewing over? The following is far from an exhaustive list but offers some ingredients worth putting in the pot.

ACCOMPLISHMENTS OF WHICH YOU ARE PARTICULARLY PROUD

As you stroll down memory lane, identify moments you're especially proud of. Earmark them in your mind and own them. Did you hit a revenue target everyone said was impossible? Did you mentor a younger employee who later became a manager? Did you achieve the position you spent years working toward? Did you become salesperson of the year or successfully launch a business? Was your company acquired, or were you part of an initial public offering? Did your employer recognize you for a unique contribution? These, and other accomplishments like them, are certainly worth remembering.

Keep in mind that not every accomplishment worth remembering has to be grand. Small successes are worth recalling too. When I started my second company, I celebrated issuing my first invoice, then the fifth, the tenth, and so on. Mom-and-pop businesses often frame the first dollar they earn. They may have big hopes for the future of their fledgling business, but they still choose to rejoice in the small start—their first sale. Their sense of satisfaction is even sweeter years later when they erect a sign that reads "Serving our community for 75 years."

Milestones—career path markers—come in all sizes.

No matter how you feel about your career today, there must have been things you did along the way that give you a sense of pleasure and contentment. Dig through your memory bank to find them, then paste them in the scrapbook of your mind. Let them serve as reminders of your successes, no matter how small, over the years.

PEOPLE YOU'VE MET ALONG THE WAY

When you reflect on your career accomplishments, I hope you also remember the important people you've met along the way. If you're like me, you can easily recall a few names without much effort.

My list includes no fewer than five: George Davis, the youth pastor I met in the town where I grew up, who played a key role in altering the trajectory of my life; Ben Wikramanayake, my manager at the bank where I worked, who exemplified the qualities of a true leader; Michelle Patterson, who recognized that the skills I developed for ministry were transferable to a sales role at Robert Half International; Dave Schnitt, who understood that one didn't need to be a CPA to sell accounting and finance services; and Sandra Bensworth, my coworker at Resources Global Professionals who suggested we start our own business, which turned out to be the best career decision I ever made.

When I look back on my career, I find that the most significant moments are often tied to the unique individuals I encountered on the journey. Without those encounters, who can say what my accomplishments would've looked like or if they would've existed at all?

In fact, when you really think about it, who we've become and what we've accomplished are rarely, if ever, solo efforts. There is always someone else who has played a part. Many have helped us navigate our career path. We are all, in some way, "standing on the shoulders of giants," meaning we have benefited from the knowledge, achievements, and influence of those who came before us.

In his book *Where Good Ideas Come From: The Natural History of Innovation*, Steven Johnson explains that good ideas do not exist independently of others' contributions: "Good ideas are not conjured out of thin air; they are built out of a collection of existing parts, the composition of which expands over time."[1] True scientists understand that any discovery they make is connected to the work of others, and they would be remiss to claim full credit for it. Johnson's survey revealed that scientists rarely, if ever, experience a flash of inspiration alone in a lab. Instead, insights often occur while collaborating with others and discussing ideas.

There can only be one original; everything that follows is built upon what came first. As Solomon said, "There is nothing new under the sun" (Ecclesiastes 1:9). We all borrow from and build upon the achievements of others. Likewise, we are all, in part, indebted to someone else for our career accomplishments.

So when you take time to reflect, make sure you spend ample time dwelling on—and appreciating—the people who have contributed to your achievements and left an imprint on the professional you have become.

RISKS TAKEN THAT HAVE ENDED IN REWARDS REAPED OR LESSONS LEARNED

The bold reap rewards from their willingness to take risks. That's just how it is—and how it should be. If someone is daring enough to take a chance and something great comes of it, they've earned it. More power to them.

If you're fortunate enough to have moments where you took a risk and something positive resulted, you deserve to revel in those successes. However, be careful not to let the pleasure derived from such good fortune turn into smug satisfaction, where past achievements prevent you from striving toward future goals.

You should focus less on what you have already accomplished and more on what you are going to do. Be like Gérard Bertrand, who is "still very much in forward motion." Always look ahead. Always envision what's next. Always think about new exploits. Always see new horizons. Always strive to reach new milestones. Always chart new courses. The goal of retirement is not to lounge around and enjoy feeding on the grass of inactivity. Past achievements are not meant to cement you in your "glory days"; they are meant to remind you that, when you apply yourself, you are capable of achieving whatever you set out to do.

Not only should you reflect on what has ended well, but you should also consider efforts that ended in failure and taught you a valuable lesson. By now, you've read many famous quotes on this subject: "Failure is simply the opportunity to begin again, this time more intelligently" (Henry Ford); "Failure is a great teacher, and, if you are open to it, every mistake has a lesson to offer" (Oprah Winfrey); "I have not failed. I've just found ten thousand ways that won't work" (Thomas A. Edison); and the like.

Interestingly, I found it challenging to locate these quotes in specific written sources. They are attributed to these figures because they have been widely spoken and written about over the course of their careers. Given their lives and the challenges they faced, we can imagine them expressing these sentiments. They never let the past be an indication of future performance.

A young entrepreneur stepped into the *Shark Tank* to pitch her business idea to the panel of experienced business professionals, the sharks. Their teeth are always sharp and ready to shred unsuspecting victims—a shark is a shark, after all.

When questioned about a spike in revenue during her first year of business, she admitted it stemmed from a mistake that turned into a blessing in disguise. She had failed to patent a T-shirt design, and another company stole her idea, marketed it to a large retailer, who then sold it in their stores. Unfortunately, the company that took her idea did not technically break the law.

With few options, she took pictures of the merchandise with her design displayed in the store and then turned to social media. She also expressed her concerns to the retailer, who agreed to stop selling the merchandise. Ultimately, her actions attracted attention, increased traffic to her website, and led to a surge in sales. That year ended profitably, and she averted a potential business-ending disaster.

Still, this young entrepreneur had made a significant mistake. Not patenting her design put her company at risk. However, the failure taught her a valuable lesson about protecting her intellectual property—and her business interests in general.

Most people understand that mistakes happen, and we fail, but that doesn't mean we need to repeat our mistakes. Mistakes can be one-time events. Failure need not be a treadmill we walk forever, nor does it have to be a frightful fiend that follows and haunts us for the rest of our days. When approached correctly, a screwup should propel us beyond it. Otherwise, it carries an air of madness; dwell on it too long, and it will drive you crazy. When it comes to failure, the best approach is to learn from it, let it go, and move on as quickly as possible. Every failure needs a full stop, a "The End," a conclusion to the story.

MEMORABLE EVENTS THAT IMPACTED YOUR CAREER—GOOD OR BAD

Every career journey involves episodes, events, or groups of events that occur as part of a larger sequence. Along the way, both good and bad things happen: your job gets outsourced to another country or relocated to another state; you are downsized or part of a reduction in force (RIF); the company you work for is acquired, and your role is eliminated; you receive a raise or a promotion; your business development efforts finally pay off, and you land a major client; or a recruiter contacts you about a job with better pay, a more attractive commission plan, and improved benefits, leading you to decide to take it.

Some people will tell you that getting fired from their job was the best thing that ever happened to them. It led to the next great chapter of their journey. Steve Jobs, for example, was fired from Apple after losing a boardroom battle with John Sculley. He went on to found NeXT, which he later sold to Apple for $400 million. Shortly thereafter, he was reappointed CEO at Apple, and, as they say, the rest is history.

Much has occurred since you embarked on your career. Whether good or bad, all experiences are worth reflecting on because, in one way or another, they have led you to where you are today, both in your career and in your life. To better appreciate your current position, you must value every step and misstep along the way, all of which should inspire you to think about where you could go from here.

MISSED OPPORTUNITIES—REGRETS

You're probably thinking, *Who in their right mind wants to invest time thinking about what might have been, what could have been, or what should have been?* Missed opportunities, especially golden ones, can be painful.

However, the sting of a missed opportunity is worth remembering. Reliving it can remind you of a feeling you'd prefer not to experience again. The trick is not to let the painful memory become like the suffering endured by Prometheus, who faced eternal torment for defying Zeus. According to the myth, an eagle ate Prometheus's liver every day, only for it to regenerate each night, causing him to experience the same agonizing pain repeatedly. Instead, the goal should be to reflect on the agony of a failed moment only as a reminder never to pass up any favorable possibilities with your name on it.

Have you ever met someone who is stuck in their career because they believe they've missed their one shot at something big—an opportunity that would have made them a huge success and change everything? They're stuck only because they never moved beyond the missed opportunity and chose rather to reinforce their negative mind-set with self-fulfilling prophecies like "Nothing ever goes my way," "There's a black cloud following me," and "Some people have all the luck, just not me."

The problem with this way of thinking is the emphasis on having only "one shot." These individuals are convinced that another opportunity will never come. They can't imagine getting another chance—another chance to make up for what they failed to do, another chance to get it right, another chance to take a risk.

(This is probably a good time to remind you of Mark Manson's theory about what is and isn't worth giving a f*ck about. When it comes to missed opportunities—even golden ones—and every other mistake we may have made in our careers and lives, you cannot allow yourself to dwell on them for an extended period. As mentioned earlier, ruminating too long over mistakes will drive you crazy. The sooner you let them go, the better. Say to yourself, *F*ck it*, and move on.)

People who don't do this are never quite ready for the next opportunity when it presents itself, even if it lands in their lap, as many opportunities do. They're so preoccupied with their past blunders that they can't see when a new chance to take a "kick at the can" arrives.

When you take time to reminisce about the five types of memories noted above, you end up getting reintroduced to yourself. As you reflect on what you've accomplished, what you failed to do, and everything in between, you'll catch glimpses of what makes you *you*. You'll see yourself in the stories being reflected upon because you are the main character in each episode. A historical overview of your career— every positive and negative step—serves as a mirror reflecting the image of who you were, who you've become, and who you are now. As I discussed in chapter 3, remembering who you are helps you either reconnect and reprise your true self or make the deliberate choice to reinvent yourself for whatever you wish to pursue—and become—in your "later period."

A bit philosophical, I know. But not as abstract and esoteric as you might think. We all have the capacity for healthy introspection, though sadly, many have not learned the joy of solitude that leads to it. For many, introspection proves to be a challenge.

Those of us who have worked for forty-plus years have grown accustomed to the hamster wheel we tread. And many don't know how to get off it. Our routine is set in stone: go to work, do our job, go home, eat, go to bed, wake up the next morning, and do it all over again. Incorporating something foreign into that routine, like moments for reflection, would be a shock to our standard operating procedure.

Our life and work life are set on cruise control, so most of us don't take or make time to remember, reminisce, and reflect. Many have no clue how.

If you're like me, however, you've begun to notice how musing seems to happen naturally as you age, without even trying. At times, you may find yourself staring off into space, drifting into a dream state, indulging in a bit of fantasy, or imagining different scenarios for yourself. Thoughts like *What if I* and *Maybe I could* may fill your mind. Great! Feed that; foster that. If thinking like that was good enough for Picasso during his surrealist period, then it's good enough for you at any time.

But you can also supplement that natural tendency by carving out time in your day to do it. "It's vital to create space in each day to let your thoughts wander beyond your imme-diate job responsibilities,"[2] says Bob Iger in his book *The Ride of a Lifetime*. Healthy reminiscing can be more than a natural tendency of aging; it can be a habit, a discipline you develop and live by. To help cultivate that, you just need a little time and a willingness to be a bit mystical. "A three-minute meditation every day may change your life: It is the gateway drug to slowing down,"[3] says Anne Lamott in her book *Almost Everything: Notes on Hope.*

Mysticism is often misunderstood because it sounds like a religious term, but that doesn't make it a bad word. Let me explain.

For many, being mystical conjures up images of those who chant, rub prayer beads, kneel on prayer mats, and live cloistered lives. Meister Eckhart, Teresa of Avila, and Saint John of the Cross come to mind. They, and other mystics like them, tapped into a range of religious practices to connect with the divine, a higher power, or the transcendent.

While this is an accurate perspective, it's only one way of looking at the word. The etymology of the word also offers a definition stripped of religious connotations. The Greek word from which it stems, *muein*, means to close one's eyes and/or lips. In other words, shutting out the world by closing your eyes and not talking are prerequisites to getting in tune with anything or anyone: nature, your feelings, a vibe, a higher power, or even yourself. Being mystical is simply the act of being contemplative, and the formula is simple: close your eyes, shut your mouth, and listen.

Anyone can do this, should they choose to make time for it.

This does not require attendance at a church, synagogue, mosque, or any other house of worship. Of course, it can be done there, but it can also be done in the sanctuary of nature, the temple of your kitchen, the cathedral of your mind, or the shrine of your automobile—anywhere, really.

Mythologists have noted how myths from different cultures emphasize the importance of mysticism. Many of the stories suggest isolating oneself in a walled garden—a place of quiet retreat to restore your soul, be introspective, and allow your mind to wander. Doing so creates an atmosphere for messages to reach you. In other words, when we adopt a contemplative posture, we open a passageway for "communications" to penetrate the noise that normally surrounds us.

So, as you consider the "last leg" of your career, add a small block of time to your daily routine for contemplation to reinforce what may already be happening naturally due to age. Being mystical, as defined above, will aid you in figuring out where your vintage career vehicle can next take you. Do yourself a favor and take a stroll down memory lane, relax, reminisce, and reflect for a bit, but don't park there too long.

CAREER MECHANICS INSPECT THE MECHANICS

RECOGNIZE THE ISSUES

ENGAGE IN CONVERSATION WITH INDIVIDUALS who dedicate their time and money to restoring "vintage" cars, and they'll likely mention that the related problems can be categorized into internal problems related to cooling systems, brakes, engines, wheels, or suspensions, and external problems such as paint damage.

Skilled mechanics identify car problems because they inspect its internal workings. So let's take a look under the hood to learn about potential problem areas. As we do, let's keep in mind the encouraging words from an article by Righter's Auto Repair entitled "Five Common Problems with Classic Cars You Should Expect": "The good news is that all of these problems can be fixed and even avoided if you have [taken the time to] address age-related issues."[1]

The Classic Car Club of America defines a classic car as a "fine" or "distinctive" automobile built between 1915 and 1948. Based on that date range, it's safe to assume that the driving conditions of today were not a consideration when those cars were manufactured. In the 1930s, for example, the speed limit ranged from twenty-five to thirty-five miles per hour in rural areas and ranged a bit less in urban areas; engines built then couldn't handle today's speed limits or the more unpredictable nature of today's driving conditions. Similarly, the materials used in cars back then differ from those used in modern vehicles and would struggle to meet the demands of today's fast and furious roads.

The reasons for driving back then were different as well. We need only recall the Sunday driver who never rushed to go anywhere; he or she happily took leisurely drives. Motorists today seldom, if ever, go for relaxed, unhurried rides. Instead, they maniacally bob and weave through traffic to reach a destination as fast as possible, only to get back in their car to do it again and again, always in the same rushed fashion.

Unlike the classics, today's autos are manufactured with advanced high-strength steel (AHSS), aluminum, plastic, composite materials, fiberglass, and carbon-fiber-reinforced polymers. You might say they are equipped to handle life in the fast lane of the twenty-first century.

The car of today is manufactured with today's roads—and our revved-up lifestyles—in mind. Buy a car now, and it comes equipped with advanced safety features, such as lane departure warning, automatic braking, blind-spot monitoring, and cameras. It comes standard with infotainment systems, keyless entry, fuel efficiency technology, advanced lighting systems, and driver assistance systems that help with automatic parking. Some even have semiautomatic driving capabilities.

In a nutshell, automobiles now reflect our technological advancements. Today's car is a microcosm of the technological environment that daily surrounds us—the milieu in which we live, breathe, and make our living. Each day you enter the workplace, you step into an environment and culture primed to improve itself through technology.

The topic of advances in technology has been and continues to be addressed everywhere: universities, workplaces, homes, boardrooms, and elsewhere. It's referenced here only to note that those advances, admirable and valuable as they may be, come with a price tag. As Aldous Huxley said in a lecture called "Over-Organization," "Many historians, many sociologists and psychologists have written at length, and with deep concern, about the price that Western man [and woman] has had to pay and will go on paying for technological progress."[2]

Suffice it to say, this progress puts the burden to "keep up" on an employee's shoulders. Regardless of how hard we may try to keep pace, at what point, I wonder, will the rapidity of advancements outpace us and leave us in a wake of digital dust? Surely, many of us in the latter stages of our careers are already covered with it.

Today's freeways, roads, and streets are challenging enough; getting around can be a stressful affair. But today's employee is also forced to travel the superhighways of the internet—at home and at the office. A zillion sites in cyberspace exist, and we have a zillion reasons to visit them, and today's technological advancements allow us to get there at warp speed.

Couple this with the "whatnot" life brings our way, and it's no wonder we overheat. The combination of stress at work and the stress of life can be overwhelming. Maybe you can relate.

Ask yourself, What makes your engine overheat? Here's a small sample of what makes mine boil: bills, bureaucracy, and bullshit; gas prices, a flat tire, and a disgruntled vendor; plumbing problems; being emotionally drained by social media; too many streaming options; poor Wi-Fi at a restaurant; politics, pundits, and pompous pop stars; and a tsunami or tornado that reminds me of how cruel, cold, and callous nature—and life—can be. Sometimes life can really grind your gears.

Work-related issues, too, like a bad boss or how your career has not turned out as you had hoped, can also cause you to overheat. The old nine-to-five can certainly make you blow a gasket.

Thanks in large part to technology, the Average Joe lives and works at too rapid a pace, often without a break. Most of us stay "connected" technologically even after the workday has officially ended. You would think that, as essential as it is to our well-being, we would have learned by now how to "cool our jets," but we haven't. We live in a state of career hyperthermia.

But overheating is only one issue. Many older vehicles also lack dashboard warning lights, often leaving their drivers unaware that the car has brake issues. The vehicle may not stop when it should—and that's an accident waiting to happen. While it's great that an older vehicle may still have plenty of get-up-and-go, if it can't stop when it needs to, the ride won't be enjoyable for long.

People can be like that too—sometimes they just don't know when or how to slow down. All revved up and constantly on the move, they rush from one place to the next, never pausing, always in a hurry. But we all know you can't live life stuck in overdrive. And if you're speeding around with faulty brakes, it's only a matter of time before you crash

Older vehicles—and older people—can't race at such a breakneck pace. Nor are they meant to. It has nothing to do with whether the engine can reach the right temperature to function well—it still can. And it has nothing to do with whether the car can get from point A to point B—it's still capable of that too. No issues exist with the car's combustion process per se; all cylinders are firing. It's simply that cars, and people—especially the vintage ones—are not built for such rapid speeds for extended periods of time, racing around like Mario Andretti, without a pit stop.

All engines need to idle, rest, and shut down.

Idling allows an engine to maintain a consistent temperature. In turn, the car is prepared for optimal performance when one is ready to drive. It also powers essential systems, such as air conditioning, heating, and other electronic components—and does so without draining the battery. Idling, as well as turning off the engine—letting it rest—allows it to cool down, which reduces wear and tear on a vehicle. High-speed driving, on the other hand, puts excessive strain on an engine and its parts.

Older cars can't bear the excessive wear and tear they once did. Hard driving and tough conditions can lead to oil leaks and burning. Sometimes it gets so bad that blue exhaust comes out of the tailpipe, a sure sign the car is "sick."

To prevent sickness, cars need motor oil. It is the lifeblood of the engine and promotes the vehicle's overall health by acting as a cleaning agent that sweeps away dirt, debris, and contaminants. Oil also acts as a barrier between the engine's moving parts. By coating metal surfaces, appropriate oil levels prevent corrosion. If leaks and burning develop and remain unaddressed, the potential for engine problems will only increase.

Look at it like this: among other things, low or nonexistent oil levels will negatively impact performance and fuel consumption and damage engine parts. Oil level "neglect" decreases lubrication within a car's engine. Decreased lubrication leads to increased friction, and increased friction—metal-on-metal rubbing—causes knocking and ticking noises, signs that the engine isn't doing well. Conversely, proper oil levels reduce both the heat generated by the engine and the friction between its parts.

Many in the latter stage of their career feel "overheated" because they experience way too much "friction" at work and elsewhere. If so, one must consider what can be done at this stage of their career journey to keep their system—mind, body, and spirit—sufficiently "lubed up."

A car, no matter its age, also cannot function optimally if it has problems with its tires and suspension. Worn-out tires mean less traction and proper handling, and shock absorbers that function poorly make for a bumpy ride. On the flip side, tires with deep treads and properly working suspension parts, like dampers and springs, afford the driver a safer—and smoother—ride; both help the vehicle cope with challenging road conditions.

Navigating one's work world is no easy task; its roads are rife with driving hazards: "potholes," "uneven surfaces," and "unclear signs." For those of us in the latter stage of our careers, this should come as no surprise. We've been around the block more than once. We are road warriors and have experienced our fair share of "driving dangers."

Take layoffs, for example. They happen all the time. According to an article by Nerdwallet, 1,186 companies administered layoffs in 2023, impacting 262,682 employees—much more than the 164,969 laid off in 2022. The culprits—or should we say "usual suspects"? —included Amazon (27,410), Meta (21,000), Google (12,115), Microsoft (11,158), and other well-known technology companies. And 2024 has followed the trend; 39,496 were laid off in the first two months, with Cisco leading the charge with 4,000 layoffs.[3]

What about outsourcing? The shift in that direction has been happening for some time. Why? Because, as KPMG's website declares, "Outsourcing done well delivers results, improves service experience, and achieves strategic business expectations."[4]

Allow me to translate: outsourced labor—whether overseas or with a national or local firm capitalizing on a shared service platform—is more cost-effective. It improves the bottom line while simultaneously accomplishing other business objectives. KPMG wants you to know that the benefits of outsourcing go beyond cost savings alone. *Its* outsourcing model also delivers enterprise-wide value in relation to capacity, compliance, continuity, and community. You may be downsized in the process, but hey, that's business, right?

Yes, it is—and it should come as no surprise. That's the nature of the beast, and as mentioned earlier, understanding its nature better prepares you to engage with it effectively. By now, you should know that in a capitalistic society, the bottom line is the top priority.

Sometimes, for a company to "make it rain"—that is, to be profitable and make money—they need to cut payroll costs, and outsourcing does just that. Unfortunately, the kind of "rain" the company makes can also bring a storm to you personally—in other words, saving on payroll might cost you your job. No one is immune: business raindrops fall on everyone; they don't discriminate.

The real question with all this, however, is not whether you will encounter such challenges but whether you are equipped to handle them when they present themselves. Do the tires on your vintage career vehicle have ample tread for safe navigation, and can its suspension absorb bumps in the road?

Lastly, and this is purely an external matter, paint damage makes a vehicle look "old." Chips, peeling, and fading are telltale signs; they reflect the relentless effects of time, every passing second leaving its mark.

You likely already know this: no one can outrun time; it inevitably catches up with us all. Still, do what you can to lessen its impact—both inside and out. As the saying goes, "If the barn [or car] needs painting . . ."

It does no good to deny the reality of the role time plays in your career and life. Ultimately, it has its way with us all. As Marcus Aurelius said, "Time is a sort of river of passing events, and strong is its current; no sooner is a thing brought to sight than it is swept by and another takes its place, and this too will be swept away." So don't waste a single second railing against the inevitable.

The restoration of a classic car requires taking a hard look at both the inside—the engine and parts under the hood— and the outside. It also demands we deal in reality, acknowledging problem areas we find and thinking through what can be done about them.

Organizations use key performance indicators (KPIs), quantifiable measures that evaluate the health of their business. The purposes of KPIs include the following.

- **Measuring Performance:** KPIs benchmark progress toward meeting company goals, such as revenue generation, cost reduction, and operational efficiency.
- **Goal Alignment:** KPIs help ensure that all departments remain aligned with the company's business strategy and objectives.
- **Decision-Making Support:** KPIs provide actionable insights by highlighting areas where the company is performing well or underperforming.
- **Accountability:** KPIs set clear expectations and responsibilities for individuals and teams, helping to track performance effectively.
- **Resource Optimization:** KPIs help determine resource needs—people, time, budget—for the company's focus areas.
- **Motivation:** KPIs give employees clear goals and targets. When linked to rewards, milestones can become powerful motivators.
- **Continuous Improvement:** KPIs allow companies to regularly assess and adjust strategies to accommodate macroeconomic changes, enhance processes, and stay competitive.

Similarly, you should establish personal KPIs to monitor your progress as you navigate the final third of your career. Set performance benchmarks, refresh your goals, collect data to make informed decisions, take responsibility for your career choices, determine the resources you need to accomplish your goals, set up a reward system for reaching milestones, and "assess and adjust" daily.

Skilled "career mechanics" take time to diagnose potential issues by inspecting the internal workings of their career "vehicle" and fixing what needs attention. Open the hood and take a hard look at the engine and its parts, while also inspecting the exterior for any wear and tear. Identify any problem areas noted earlier, then grab your tools and get to work.

7
HAND ME A WRENCH

REPAIRS ARE A REALITY

Now that we've taken a closer look at the problem areas of vintage rides, let's turn to the corrective measures that can be taken in relation to them. In other words, what can you do to ensure your classic career vehicle's engine continues to purr, growl, and hum? The truth is, vehicle complications will continue to occur, especially if the restoration-and-repair process does not keep up with the effects of time. So, what are some tools you can use to help in this process?

Implied in the preceding chapter are four tools for classic vehicle repair: Slow Your Roll (prevent overheating), Discard Discord (reduce friction), Embrace Newness (repair or replace broken or faulty parts), and Stay Grounded (replace worn-out tires).

SLOW YOUR ROLL

When I say "slow your roll," here's what I mean: be mindful, take a step back, pause, calm down, linger in moments, create mental space for yourself, relax, take it easy, practice patience, be composed, smell the roses, and do the opposite of whatever causes you to overheat. In a nutshell, implement approaches that reduce or eliminate stress and friction.

Work demands a lot from you. And certainly, there are times in your career when you must push your career vehicle harder, so to speak. In *Star Trek*, Captain James T. Kirk often asked the engine room for more power to propel the Starship Enterprise beyond its normal limits. Likewise, in your career, there will be occasions when you'll need to do the same. Career heroes who set high but achievable goals push themselves until they reach them. Granted.

At this stage, however, it is important to remember that you can only push so hard. Scotty, the Enterprise's engineer, often responded to Kirk with, "I'm giving her all she's got, Captain." Kirk needed to be reminded that an engine has its limits.

My suggestion to slow your roll, however, need not be at the expense of a continual striving toward goals, which one should have regardless of the career stage they find themselves in. Slowing down need not be at the expense of accomplishing things. The recommendation is more of an admonishment to better define the extent of one's striving.

Somewhere along the way, we convinced ourselves of the need to work seventy-hour workweeks and be dialed in 24-7, believing that doing so leads to success. That mentality is what caused Arianna Huffington to collapse from exhaustion. The launch and continued success of *The Huffington Post* had placed far too many demands on her career engine, leading her to collapse and hit her head on her desk. She ended up on the floor of her office in a pool of blood. Her "engine room" finally spoke up, saying, "We've given all she's got, Captain. There's nothing left to give."

Huffington recounts this tale in her book *Thrive* and says it led to a long-overdue wake-up call. Safe to assume money was no longer an issue for her: *The Huffington Post* had been acquired by AOL in 2011 for $315 million. She had also attained a position of power in her field and received ample recognition: she'd made it to the cover of *Time* as one of the world's Most Influential People. Nevertheless, her collapse forced her to reassess her definition of success. "In terms of the traditional measures of success, which focus on money and power, I was very successful," she says. "But I was not living a successful life by any sane definition of success."[1]

So how does Huffington now define success? By what metrics does she measure it? She offers one answer pertinent to our discussion: well-being. In fact, compared to the other metrics she now uses to define success, like wisdom and wonder, she devotes more pages to it. And because most of us are tempted to use money and power to gauge our own success, she tells us: "The architecture of how we live our lives is badly in need of *renovation and repair*" (italics mine).[2]

Huffington and I agree on one way to cultivate our well-being: meditation and/or being mystical, a word which, as I sought to clarify in chapter 5, is less religious-sounding than one may think. Even on that point, we agree. That's why she titles a section in her chapter on well-being "Meditation: It's Not Just for Enlightenment Anymore."[3]

As elaborated upon in chapter 5, being mystical and meditative are disciplines—developed habits and codes of behavior—that can be practiced anytime, anywhere. It does not require attendance at a church, mosque, cathedral, temple, shrine, or any other building dedicated to religious beliefs, though some find this helpful. Nor do you need to wander in nature, although being outdoors amid the sounds, stillness, and solitude of it can lend itself to contemplation and reflection. And you don't need to chant, rub prayer beads, or kneel on a prayer mat. But again, if that works for you, have at it. Mysticism can be practiced anywhere.

Opposite of what you may think, when it comes to meditation, nothing is required of you per se. You only need to be, not do.

Maybe you're familiar with the scene in *Forgetting Sarah Marshall* where Chuck, played by Paul Rudd, attempts to teach Peter Bretter, played by Jason Segel, how to surf. Chuck, who calls himself Kunu to sound more Hawaiian, takes a Zen-like approach with his student. When it comes to surfing, Kunu says, "Don't do anything. Don't try to surf. Don't do it. The less you do, the more you do."

Of course, when Peter does absolutely nothing, Kunu tells him he must do more than that. By the end of the lesson, it's clear Peter is a bit confused and has not found the balance of doing more by doing less.

The mystics who surf, those who train themselves to catch meditative waves, understand mysticism doesn't require anything except being still—and dwelling for a period of time in that stillness. That's when—and where—the magic happens.

Mysticism matters because it is critical to your well-being. Moments of solitude and introspection clear away the detritus that can gather within your heart and mind over the days, weeks, months, even years if allowed. And as that "trash" builds up, it becomes harder and harder to be in the moment, to be present, and to focus on what the day has in store for you.

So when you're getting overheated because of the millions of things you think you need to do to ensure that your late-stage employment is a roaring success, slow your roll and do this: nothing. Take fifteen to twenty minutes out of your day and let your mind wander, wonder, and wish.

DISCARD THE DISCORD

Meditation prevents "overheating," but it also eliminates career—and life— "friction." It offers reprieve from the grind of work and life that can rob you of a sense of well-being.

But what more can be done to remove the friction in your career and life? What can you do to discard the discord? How do you lubricate your career engine? How do you eliminate or minimize sources of career conflict, disharmony, and negativity?

The following suggestions should prove helpful but are far from an exhaustive list: silence your inner critic, give yourself a break, challenge the negative ads in your mind, cultivate positive self-talk, and stay in your lane, which requires recognizing the importance of work-life balance, learning to say no, equalizing action and reflection, and being intentional in your choice of involvements.

- **Silence your inner critic.** More often than not, the loudest, most friction-producing sounds we hear come from within, where our inner critic whispers its harsh, adversarial words to our heart and mind. Arianna Huffington calls it "the obnoxious roommate living in our head."[4]

  Let's keep it real for a moment. Any honest review of one's career and life—one's history—reveals a field full of imperfection, a crop of maddening miscellaneous mistakes made over a span of years: opportunities missed, talents and gifts misapplied, misguided motivations, misinterpreted market "signs," career missteps, and other times when we just flat-out missed the mark.

And when our inner critic wants to remind us of these errors and failures—which, by the way, it tends to do when we are in a meditative state—here's what you might hear:

- "You're not getting that opportunity back. That train has left the station."
- "You were passed up for that position because you are past your prime."
- "You've got nothing left to offer. Your skills are obsolete."
- "Admit it. You're too old. That job is best filled by a young person."
- "Give it up; throw in the towel."
- "Quit fooling yourself. You're not as sharp as you once were."
- "Clearly, you've lost a step. Others can work circles around you."
- "At your age . . . and your salary . . . no one's going to hire you."

Negative self-talk like this creates late-stage career friction, and that sort of noise will discourage you from maintaining and participating in an active work life. It will convince you that you have nothing left to contribute and will hamstring your sense of usefulness. If your inner critic is left to speak its mind in this manner, your forward progress will stop.

Another way to reduce the friction in your classic career vehicle is by doing the following.

- **Give yourself a break.** No one is perfect. Read that again. Do yourself a favor and realize that this applies to you as well; free yourself from the burden of perfectionism. So you've made some mistakes. You've dropped the ball. Your career, or worse yet, your life, is a mess. Offer yourself some compassion and grace, and move on.

  Nothing holds us back more than our preoccupation with past mistakes. Until you get over it—accepting that you've made mistakes and letting them go—you remain time bound in an event you can no longer change. I know this is all Psych 101 stuff, but until you actually do it . . .

To keep your vintage model lubed up, so to speak, you can also do the following:

- **Challenge the negative ads in your mind.** They'll keep popping up until you do. Here's a prescription to follow: write down each negative comment made by your inner critic, and then highlight any evidence to the contrary. For example, counter *You're too old* with *Look at Warren Buffett* and *At seventy-four, Bruce Springsteen still tours and does three-hour shows.* Counter *You have nothing left to offer the company* with *I know more about its operations than anyone else*. In other words, rather than wasting time giving credence to the negative ad, consider its flip side. Turn it on its head. Don't accept the negativity as gospel. Challenge its validity; rebuff its ridiculousness.

Doing the inverse—highlighting positive ads in your mind—is like keeping your oil levels in check. It's essential for smooth, frictionless performance.

- **Cultivate positive self-talk.** Tom Rath and Donald O. Clifton wrote a *New York Times* best seller called *How Full Is Your Bucket?* on this very topic. The long and short of the book, based on the metaphor of a bucket and a dipper, is that negativity kills and positivity enlivens. Every person has an invisible bucket that is emptied or filled, depending on what others say and do to us. Each person also has an invisible dipper. "When we use that dipper to fill other people's buckets—by saying and doing things to increase their positive emotions—we also fill our own buckets" (italics mine).[5]

What Rath and Clifton say about the positive and negative effects of others also applies to what we say and do to ourselves. Their research emphasizes how "negative emotions can be harmful to your health and might even shorten your life . . . [and] . . . positive emotions are an essential daily requirement for survival."[6]

Bottom line: don't let your inner critic crash your party and talk trash about you. Equip yourself with a meaningful substitute message—a mantra perhaps? —with which to combat your inner adversary.

- **Stay in your lane and set clear boundaries for yourself.** Dirty Harry, played by Clint Eastwood in the film *Magnum Force*, said some memorable words that those in the latter stage of their career would do well to remember: "A man's got to know his limitations." In the workplace, that means focusing on your assumed responsibilities and avoiding issues and tasks outside your scope of expertise or job duties. In general, it suggests avoiding overcommitting more than is necessary or even feasible. For our purposes, it's a reminder you can't do everything.

  As you age, the fact of the matter is you just can't do everything you once did. Nor should you try to. This is not an admission of defeat; it's a recognition that you've changed. At every stage, but especially in a career's final stage, you must be honest with yourself about the current state of your capabilities.

  Sometimes that means **taking a step down the corporate ladder.**

Many figure that an employee must, throughout the span of their career, move up the corporate ladder, never down. "We assume and believe," says Tess Vigeland in her book *Leap: Leaving a Job With No Plan B to Find the Career and Life You Really Want*, "that every step on the career ladder must and will be an upward trajectory."[7] But taking steps down the corporate ladder can be a way to better align yourself with who you are, at any stage in your vocational evolution. It can reposition you into a "restorative niche" and allow you to be more in sync with your true self, your gifts, and your talents.[8]

Executives in particular are prone to being boxed into thinking they must always rise to the role above the one they currently occupy. Because today's work culture expects people always to be climbing, they mistakenly think taking a position with less responsibility, or one that seems like a demotion, makes no sense. As Barbara Mitchell says in an article entitled "Stepping Back Down the Ladder," "Unfortunately, many organizations put people in 'boxes' and have difficulty understanding that people who have been in executive positions can be satisfied taking a role in which they won't be in charge."[9]

The same holds true, however, no matter what level of position you hold within a company. Regardless of the role, you may reach a point when you want to step down or step back because it better suits you to do so: finding the right fit has become more important than the prestige, power, and money—superficial rewards—afforded by a position. It's possible you have come to the same conclusion as Alice in Lewis Carroll's *Wonderland* tale, who said, "I've got to get back to my right size."[10] Sometimes stepping down is a matter of rightsizing yourself, a shift that better enables you to thrive, regardless of what others may think of your decision to do so.

Staying in your lane also means **fighting for work-life balance.**

The pedal need not always be to the metal. Your vintage career vehicle should not remain fixed in fifth gear. Letting it idle a bit, even turning it off, will prevent potential problems. Remember Arianna Huffington.

In her book *A Short Guide to a Happy Life*, Anna Quindlen offers a treasure trove of homespun wisdom about what is truly important in life and what generates genuine happiness.

In it, she reminds readers, "You cannot be really first-rate at your work if your work is all you are."[11] She advises us to "get a life," meaning "a real life, not a manic pursuit of the next promotion, the bigger paycheck, the larger house."[12] None of those things matter if you are lying in a pool of blood in your office because you banged your head on your desk after fainting from exhaustion. As they say, if you don't have your health, you have nothing.

At this phase in your career, you must know when to say, "I've done all I can do today; the rest will have to wait until tomorrow," and "I've spent enough hours in the office this week; it's time to hang out with family and friends." In other words, be present elsewhere besides work. Do not sacrifice a balanced life at the altar of work. "Your work," as Stephen M. Pollan and Mark Levine say in *Die Broke*, "[should be] what you do so you can have a life."[13]

Staying in your lane also means **learning to say no**.

N.O. No: a small word; for some, a huge challenge.

There are those who just can't refuse anyone. They're not good at saying no and end up taking on more and more projects, more and more tasks, and more and more missions. In the process, they run themselves ragged and become no good to anyone, including themselves. Perpetually doing, these busy bees have not learned the art of pushing back when already at full capacity. Their work never seems to end because when asked to do something, they always answer yes.

By saying no to others, however, you are better positioned to pursue projects, positions, and pursuits that are more aligned with your overarching professional goals.

Not veering into other lanes also means **balancing action and reflection**. Those in the latter stage of their career understand the importance of getting work done but also appreciate taking time to reflect on accomplishments, the work already done. Without reflective time, our view of the world and our position within it becomes limited. If true, it would be wise to make the appropriate investments in pausing and pondering.

More than any other character in literature, Ebenezer Scrooge, the miserly protagonist created by Charles Dickens in *A Christmas Carol,* conveys the opposite of what I am talking about.

Early in the story, Dickens portrays Scrooge as someone with a fixation on obtaining and retaining wealth. Nothing and no person can distract him from that mission. He's hell-bent. But his determination to accomplish this pursuit comes at a cost. Emptiness fills his life. He spends no time with family or friends, has no joyous moments basking in holiday celebrations, and lacks the happiness that comes from sharing his good fortune with others. Scrooge's singular focus on gain, what Dickens calls his "master passion," leaves him unaware of how limited and out of balance his life and world have become.

It takes visitations by three spirits to bring him to his senses—specters that show him the error of his ways and serve to remind him what is truly important in life. During his time with them, Scrooge is forced to reflect on the various stages of his life—who he once was and what he had become—so that he may repent and be a different person. Only then does Scrooge become someone first-rate in his work and in life. Reflection leads him to the realization that there's more to life than accumulating riches. Through reflection, he gains a deeper understanding of his place in the world.

Finally, staying in your lane requires **being intentional in your choice of involvements**. Jim Cramer, host of *Mad Money*, anchor on CNBC's *Squawk on the Street*, and author, regularly emphasizes the importance of knowing why you want to buy a particular stock. According to him, you should be able to rattle off at least three reasons why you want to purchase shares of a publicly traded company. Similarly, at this juncture in your career, it is imperative that you are able to articulate the reasons why you are in a particular job.

It may be as simple as you need to pay your bills and the job affords you a salary that covers those expenses. Or perhaps, despite the salary, the job "feeds" you in other ways: it may increase your sense of being a contributor, allow you to mentor younger employees, or provide an outlet for your gifts to shine. Maybe it just offers you a place to go every day—and that's reason enough.

The reasons, per se, do not matter; having some does. Knowing why you are doing what you are doing—the purpose behind your commitment to a course of action—provides fuel to maintain the fire of an active life of employment. Having intent will keep your vintage career vehicle operational and moving down the road.

So, as you drive through the latter stage of your work life, take note of what causes and creates discord for you. And to rid yourself of that discord—the grinding, squealing, rattling, hissing, and pinging noises of the job—put the following suggestions into practice: silence your inner critic, give yourself a break, challenge the negative ads in your mind, cultivate positive self-talk, and set clear boundaries for yourself.

EMBRACE NEWNESS

A third way to repair your vintage career vehicle is by embracing newness.

Everyone could tell. My face told the story: the pain was too much to bear. My shoulders were in such bad shape that I could no longer raise my arms above my waistline. Putting on a belt was impossible, and combing my hair, when I had it . . . fuhgeddaboudit. As it turned out, I suffered from osteo-arthritis, a condition that occurs when the protective carti-lage that cushions the ends of the bones wears down over time, leading to intense pain, stiffness, and reduced range of motion. My doctor's recommendation: shoulder replace-ment—a most unpleasant prospect to consider.

A shoulder replacement entails examinations (X-rays, MRI scans, and CT scans), being anesthetized, removing damaged upper arm bones and shoulder blades, implanting artificial parts, sutures, scars, and a dreaded recovery period that includes months of physical therapy. Oh joy!

Body parts break down, and so do the parts of your career vehicle. When they do, they often need to be replaced.

Maybe you can relate. Until now, your career has been cruising along quite nicely. Your career vehicle has absorbed the general wear and tear of your employment journey with no major issues.

But you've begun to hear some sounds you haven't heard before: the grinding and squealing of misapplied gifts and talents, rattling from loosely fitted roles, hissing from career missteps, and pinging from company decisions and demands that create disharmony, angst, and unhappiness on the job.

Perhaps the cumulative effects of work stress—the rapid pace of technological advances, the get-more-done-with-less mentality of management, increased workloads from business transformation, consolidation, and acquisition-related efforts, and more—have started to take a toll on your career auto.

It might be time to replace a few "parts" in your "career vehicle." Here are some areas you should consider inspecting:

- Outdated Engine – Obsolete skills or methods that should be updated or replaced with modern techniques
- Worn Tires – Archaic approaches or strategies that no longer provide the necessary traction to keep your career moving forward
- Rusty Transmission – Outdated communication styles and processes that negatively impact career progress
- Faded Paint Job – Antiquated ideas that affect the appeal and relevance of your work
- Aging Suspension – Out-of-date perspectives on how to handle the bumps and changes in your career journey
- Faulty Ignition System – Bygone motivations that fail to inspire you to start new projects or initiatives
- Broken Headlights – Old goals that no longer provide visibility into the career road before you

In general, it would also be helpful to replace old and outdated concepts of work itself. Do you remember the retiree in the sauna that I referenced in chapter 1? Based on his exclamation, "Thank God Almighty, I'm free at last," and the tone of it, one could assume his outlook on work was one of drudgery and toil—something he *had* to do, not something he *got* to do. Work itself seemed to hold little or no value. When that happens, "when work becomes [just] a job, its intrinsic value vanishes."[14] That mind-set—work is just a job I have to do—is as old as the hills. A healthy view of an active work life does not include that view.

Shifting away from dated views of work also requires rejecting the notion that work exists solely to earn a paycheck. As Sam Keen puts it, "When we spend the majority of our time doing work that gives us a paycheck but no sense of meaning, we inevitably get bored and depressed."[15] This isn't to say that making money—and maximizing one's time to do so—isn't important; you should aim to grow your earnings for as long as you can. Still, building a career must be about more than just a hefty bank account.

Your concept of work, especially at this phase, should also allow for an expression of your individuality. Today's hyperefficient work world can easily make you feel like part of a machine. Becoming Borg-like in the workplace erases an appreciation of your humanity, and participation in work should never be reduced to a machine-like existence.

Rather than being assimilated in such a fashion, you should strive to maintain your uniqueness. Don't let the job define who you are; define what the job becomes. Seek opportunities that allow you to be in sync with yourself, that give space for your talents and gifts, and that afford you more meaning and satisfaction. Resist being squeezed into roles designed for the masses.

This may require you to curate or craft the type of work life you desire. "There are always more options available to us than we might realize,"[16] says Rick Rubin in his mind-opening book *The Creative Act: A Way of Being*. Consider exploring new fields or roles that align with emerging trends or personal passions, even if they diverge from your current path. Practice wayfinding—the process of moving from your current position and planning a route to the next possible place.

While you're at it, take the opportunity to assess or reassess any outdated views you might have about technology. As mentioned in chapter 6 overdependence on technology can be detrimental. Excessive cruising on the superhighways of the worldwide web can rob you of time needed for contemplation and reflection. However, underdependence can have negative ramifications as well.

Why not let technology save you hours in your day? It can be used in a healthy and beneficial manner to accomplish tasks that once took much longer to do: data analytics, business intelligence, word processing summarization, identification of solutions to complex problems, automation of repetitive tasks, and more. An objective review of your relationship with tech can help you find ways to make your job—and life—easier.

You should also give thought to updating your classic career vehicle for modern driving by refining your approach to maximize impact. Enhance how you lead, manage, or work to boost both your influence and satisfaction. Focus on delegating and mentoring, involving others, and fostering collaboration rather than handling everything yourself. Small adjustments like these can make your work experience more enjoyable.

Lastly, you should jettison any obsolete ideas about what your career should or can be. Fight all employment myths that maintain that age is the determining factor in what you can do. Reject all notions that contradict a fresh vision you may have for your career at this point in time. Employment history has countless examples of individuals who have identified a new North Star and followed it.

When mulling over career moves, including those of a revolutionary nature, remember there are no hard and fast rules; you can chart your own course into something new. And assuming you have the physical capacity, age need not limit your choices. The are numerous new roads and routes to explore, if you so desire. It's not to say this would be easy, but if it puts you in a place where work now keeps you engaged, it would be worth it. Of course, bear in mind that wisdom dictates you cover all bases related to any and all personal obligations. Notwithstanding, there are times you should remake and remodel yourself, replace old parts, take on a new form, shed outdated layers of skin, and alter the structure of your career.

Embracing something new means embracing change, and that's hard to do. Change often disrupts our routines and challenges our comfort zones, making us feel unsettled. It requires us to let go of familiar patterns and adapt to new circumstances, a process that can be daunting. Our initial response may be to resist. However, change has a way of reinvigorating us, injecting fresh energy and perspective into our lives.

Opening ourselves up to new experiences stimulates growth and learning, which can lead to a renewed sense of purpose. Welcoming change can also lead to personal transformation. As we throw ourselves into new situations, we can continue to build upon the career we've developed over the years.

While the process of change can be challenging, it is often through these challenges that we find our greatest strengths and possibilities. By facing and embracing change and new situations, we position ourselves to experience growth, renewal, and a more dynamic and fulfilling late-stage career.

STAY GROUNDED

Another way to restore and repair your vintage career vehicle is to make sure its tires have deep treads. Deep treads, better traction; better traction, smoother ride.

In the movie *Days of Thunder*, Cole Trickle, portrayed by Tom Cruise, starts off with limited knowledge about race cars, being more accustomed to stock cars. He doesn't realize that race cars require a different driving technique than stock cars. Consequently, he overheats the tires, making them slick and leading to a slippery ride.

Harry Hogge, played by Robert Duvall, knows a ton about race cars. He tries to teach Cole the importance of proper tire care, stating, "Tires is what wins a race. If we can't figure you a way to run so you don't melt the damn tires, we can't finish a race."[17]

Confused, Cole asks Hogge for clarification. To demonstrate, Hogge has Cole perform test runs on the track. In his usual style, Cole's driving overheats the tires, resulting in a slippery performance. When he follows Hogge's technique, the tires stay intact, providing better traction and a smoother, faster run.

To successfully navigate the latter part of your professional journey with greater ease, it's essential to regularly check and maintain the "tire tread." Doing so offers at least four key benefits:

- **Control** – Deeper treads enhance a vehicle's responsiveness, allowing for quicker reaction times. Similarly, when navigating a career phase often marked by a sense of aimlessness, ambivalence, loss of purpose, or reluctance to explore new opportunities, maintaining control and adaptability becomes essential. Just as deeper treads provide better handling on any road, having a firm grip on your career path—no matter the conditions—is key to maneuvering toward success. It's essential to remember that personal accountability—being in control—is key to advancing your career through its latter stage.

- **Traction** – A stronger grip on the road allows you to confidently navigate your career path, regardless of the challenges—whether it's the downpour of negative economic conditions or the icy obstacles of organizational decisions, layoffs, and divestitures. Deep tire treads will keep you securely grounded and ensure you stay on track no matter what lies ahead.

- **Steering** – Steering requires having your hands firmly on the wheel. As mentioned above, in your career, taking personal responsibility to guide your path is essential, no matter the stage you're in. With the right tread depth, you can confidently steer in any direction, even if faced with new opportunities or unexpected challenges. Whether accelerating toward a goal or navigating obstacles, a strong grip ensures smoother, more controlled steering.

- **Performance** – Deep tire treads enhance vehicle performance, delivering a smoother, safer ride by reducing the risk of skidding and hydroplaning. Proper tread depth ensures consistent contact with the road, which also boosts fuel efficiency. Similarly, with the right traction, your career vehicle will go further with less effort, getting more miles per gallon on your journey, regardless of the stage you're in.

The problems associated with classic career vehicles don't have to stop you from cruising smoothly down your professional path. While the harsh realities of the working world are constant and its rough road conditions can make navigating the final stages of your career difficult, there are tools available to keep your vehicle in peak condition and help you stay on course. You can slow down by carving out time for reflection and activities outside work, learn to minimize the "noise" and "distractions" of the workplace, replace outdated habits with fresh approaches, and routinely check your tread so you remain grounded to better steer your way through your work world and handle whatever obstacles lie ahead.

CONCLUSION

IN THE MOVIE *THE INTERN*, Robert De Niro plays Ben, a bored, retired seventy-year-old. Preferring to remain active, he applies to be a senior intern at an online fashion company and secures the position. The company's founder, Jules Ostin (played by Anne Hathaway), is a driven and demanding entrepreneur. As the magic of moviemaking would have it, Ben becomes her intern, but this is far from a role in name only. Jules initially has no plans to give him meaningful work or allow access to her. To her, hiring an intern is merely for appearances. Over time, however, Ben proves not only useful but also a critical source of wisdom, knowledge, and support—becoming a valuable sounding board for the young businesswoman.

The movie contains a scene pertinent to everything discussed so far in this book, in which Ben talks about how he feels regarding his retirement. Here's what he said:

"Freud, said, 'Love and work. Work and love. That's all there is.' Well, I'm retired, and my wife is dead. As you can imagine, that's given me some time on my hands. My wife's been gone for three and a half years. I miss her in every way. And retirement? That is an ongoing relentless effort in creativity. At first, I admit I enjoyed the novelty of it. Sort of felt like playing hooky. I used all the miles I'd saved and traveled the globe. The problem was, no matter where I went, as soon as I got home, the nowhere-to-be thing hit me like a ton of bricks. I realized the key to this whole deal was to keep moving. Get up, get out of the house, and go somewhere. Anywhere."

Read those last three sentences again.

As I have argued throughout, the last thing you want is to graze on the grass of inactivity; you need to stay in your career vehicle, keep on course, and continue cruising down your employment path. Failing to do so creates a void—an emptiness filled with a sense of meaninglessness and purpose-lessness. As Pink aptly says, we should opt to drive until the wheels fall off. When they do, that's your signal to finally call it quits. Until then, stay committed to pushing the finish line further into the future.

Begin by letting go of the traditional concept of retire-ment. Instead, embrace the idea of staying active in your career, however you choose to define it. Your career is a life-long journey, so reject the mind-set that it's over just because the finish line is in sight; seeing the end doesn't mean you're there yet. And it can always be extended. The latter stage of your career is not a time to detach from the working world for good, but rather an opportunity to transition into something new, something redefined and recast. It's the time to explore fresh ways to contribute and stay engaged.

To finish strong and cross the finish line on your own terms, you'll need to reclaim your inner rebel. Get mad as hell at the employment myth that suggests you have nothing left to offer or that your usefulness has waned simply because of your age. Resist the urge to follow old playbooks, and create a new one for the road ahead. Fight the tendency to waste time and remember this: older adults have the capacity to learn well into their senior years. Think of your career as a series of evolving periods, not phases of "better" or "worse."

Aging doesn't mean your career declines—it transforms. So embrace the rebel within, and challenge the limiting beliefs that no longer serve you.

When it comes to overhauling your career, you have options. By taking time for reflection—a life and career review—you can identify ways to reprise yourself. Reprising allows you to reconnect with the person you've always been at your core, while still planning for the future you want to create.

～

Sometimes, however, simply splintering off from the overarching theme of your career isn't enough. A reprise may fall short if you've determined that a full-blown, comprehensive reinvention is necessary—if you've decided to pursue something entirely different from what you've been doing.

Whether you're refining a familiar path or forging a brand-new one by changing lanes, the key to a successful late-stage career reformation is to remain intentional and true to yourself as you navigate the road before you.

Being in the last third of your career has earned you the right to reminisce. With 90,000 to 125,000 hours of work behind you, you've surely earned the luxury of reflecting on various career moments: accomplishments you're particularly proud of, people who have impacted you, risks you've taken that resulted in either rewards or valuable lessons, and memorable events that influenced your professional journey in one way or another. Even missed opportunities—regrets—can serve as reminders not to let chances with your name on them slip by.

Do yourself a favor: take a stroll down memory lane, relax, reminisce, and reflect. But don't linger there too long. Dwelling too long on yesterday won't help when today and tomorrow—and everything they hold—are demanding your attention.

Repairing and servicing your classic career vehicle is essential to ensure it functions optimally. Whether you like it or not, age—and the wear and tear that comes with it—is a reality we all must face.

Those of us in the latter stage of our career, like classic cars, experience common issues: overheating, worn-out tires, engine problems, suspension and brake issues, and even external concerns like paint damage. That's why restoring your classic career vehicle for new roads requires a close inspection of both the interior—the engine and parts under the hood—and the exterior. However, the reality of repair work doesn't have to be daunting. Good career mechanics have the tools they need to get the job done.

You can prevent "overheating" by learning to slow your pace. Implement strategies that reduce or eliminate stress and friction. Make time for reflection and contemplation, and incorporate moments of solitude into your schedule. Let your mind wander, wonder, and wish.

To quiet the discord of work-life "noise," silence your inner critic that fixates on past missteps, missed opportunities, or moments of falling short. Instead, offer yourself grace—acknowledge your mistakes and move forward. Continuously challenge any negative thoughts playing in your mind. Replace negative messages with positive ones, and reject the notion that age limits your ability to contribute.

To further reduce friction, stay in your lane and set clear boundaries. Be honest with yourself about your limitations and the current state of your abilities. If necessary, consider stepping down on the corporate ladder. Fight for work-life balance, learn to say no, and strive for harmony between action and reflection. Stay committed to achieving goals, but also take time to appreciate your accomplishments. Above all, be intentional in the roles you select—make sure you have at least three reasons behind the work you do.

There are times with every vehicle, especially classics, when parts need to be replaced—the car sounds off and something needs to be fixed. Similarly, in the last third of your career, it's not uncommon to hear unfamiliar "noises" signaling that something isn't quite right: the grinding and squealing of misapplied gifts and talents, rattling from ill-fitting roles, hissing from career missteps, and pinging from company decisions or demands that create disharmony, angst, and unhappiness at work.

That's why it's wise to embrace new ideas and replace outdated concepts of work, such as the mind-set that work is just a job you do for a paycheck. Your view of work should reflect an expression of your individuality. At this stage, possibly more than any other, it's important to find your sweet spot where you are "optimally stimulated" and create harmony between your occupation and sense of calling. While this may require you to carefully curate and craft the type of work life you desire, it is achievable.

Also, remember to regularly check the "tire tread" of your classic career vehicle—after all, "Tires are what win the race." Sufficient tread will provide better control, traction, steering, and performance in relation to the latter stage of your career.

Even if your goal is to keep cruising until the wheels fall off, you still need traction and stability to continue moving smoothly down your career path.

The challenges that come with classic career vehicles don't have to derail your lifelong career journey. The difficulties associated with the working world will stay constant, and the rough road conditions encountered on one's career journey can make navigating the final stages difficult, the tools mentioned above can help you keep your vehicle in top condition and stay on course.

Looking back over your career, you might wonder where the time went. You've noticed that there's less road ahead than behind, and are now questioning, What can be done with the time that remains?

That's why the last third of one's career is not for the faint of heart. Difficult decisions must be made about where you can go from here and how you get there.

At the very least, regardless of what you choose to do, it should be meaningful and purposeful because time is more precious when there's less of it to waste. Reflecting on these "final days" needn't be overwhelming; doing so offers a chance to consider adjustments that could help further your career with renewed purpose. Nearing or entering this stage doesn't mean you've reached the end; approaching the end is not the same as being there.

Each phase of your career, including the final one, requires you to take responsibility for the direction in which you steer your career vehicle. This period is simply another transition point—a "hinge moment" that allows you to look thoughtfully both backward and forward. It's a chance to connect past career movements with those that have yet to occur, those you've yet to create. Instead of putting your career vehicle in park, do what you need to do to keep cruising until the wheels fall off.

GLOSSARY

Overhaul: to examine thoroughly, repair; to renovate, remake, revise, or renew thoroughly.

Rebuild: to make extensive repairs to; to make extensive changes in.

Reform: to put or change into an improved form or condition; to amend or improve by change of form or removal of faults or abuses.

Remake: to make anew or in a different form.

Remodel: to alter the structure of.

Renovate: to restore to a former better state; to restore to life, vigor, or activity.

Repair: to restore by replacing a part or putting together what is torn or broken; to restore to a sound or healthy state.

Restore: to bring back to or put back into a former or original state.

Update: to bring up to date.

NOTES

Introduction

1   Susan Cain, *Quiet: The Power of Introverts in a World That Can't Stop Talking* (New York: Crown Publishers, 2012), 125.
2   Thomas Moore, *A Life at Work: The Joy of Discovering What You Were Born To Do* (New York: Broadway Books, 2008), 45.
3   Graham Ward and Isabelle Lebbe, "Retirement Is Becoming Just the 'Third Half' of Life. Here Are the 4 Key Mindsets We've Identified Among the New Generation of Retirees," Fortune.com, March 7, 2004, https://fortune.com/2024/03/07/retirement-third-half-of-life-key-mindsets-new-generation-retirees-careers-personal-finance/.
4   Steve Lopez, "As Years Pass, the Perks of Old Age Do Add Up," *Los Angeles Times*, July 21, 2024, https://www.pressreader.com/usa/los-angeles-times-sunday/20240721/281801404203297.
5   Bill Burnett and Dave Evans, *Designing Your Life: How to Build a Well-Lived, Joyful Life* (New York: Knopf, Borzoi Books, 2016), 49.
6   Timothy Butler, *Getting Unstuck: How Dead Ends Become New Paths* (Boston: Harvard Business School Press, 2007), xv, xiv.
7   Mary Catherine Bateson, *Composing a Further Life: The Age of Active Wisdom* (New York: Knopf, 2010), 9.
8   D. Michael Lindsay, *Hinge Moments: Making the Most of Life's Transitions* (Downers Grove, IL: InterVarsity Press, 2021), 3.
9   "Pink," *60 Minutes*, interview with Cecilia Vega, season 56, episode 38, produced by Will Croxton and Brit McCandless, June 9, 2024.

Chapter 1: Let's Call It a Day

1   Sam Keen, *Fire in the Belly: On Being a Man* (New York: Bantam Books, 1992), 55.
2   Bill Burnett and Dave Evans, *Designing Your Life* (New York: Alfred A. Knopf, 2019), XXV.

3   Alan Briskin, *The Stirring of Soul in the Workplace* (San Francisco: Jossey-Bass Publishers, 1996), 195.

4   Jo Ann Jenkins, foreword to *Work Reimagined: Uncover Your Calling* by Richard J. Leider and David A. Shapiro (San Francisco: Berrett-Koehler Publishers, 2015), ix.

5   Mikael Wood, "Fleetwood Mac Songbird," *Los Angeles Times*, December 2, 2022.

6   Mikael Wood, "Fleetwood Mac Songbird."

7   Matthew McConaughey, *Greenlights* (New York: Crown, 2020), 257.

8   Peter Buckman, "I'm 78 and Refuse to Retire—Here Are 9 Things About Happiness and Money We're Often Taught Too Late," CNBC.com, September 17, 2019, https://www.cnbc.com/2019/09/17/78-year-old-who-refuses-to-retire-shares-im-portant-life-lessons-happiness-success-money.html.

9   Peter Buckman, "I'm 78 and Refuse to Retire."

10 Thomas Moore, *A Life at Work: The Joy of Discovering What You Were Born to Do* (New York: Broadway Books, 2008), 182.

11 Michel de Montaigne, *Selected Essays* (New York: International Collectors Library, 1952), 138.

12 Joseph R. Hearn, *The Bell Lap: The 8 Biggest Mistakes to Avoid as You Approach Retirement* (Omaha, NE: Provisio Publishing, 2009), viii.

Chapter 2: Resistance Is Not Futile

1   J Paul Getty, "The Art of Individuality," in Peter Krass, *The Book of Business Wisdom: Classic Writings by the Legends of Commerce and Industry* (New York: John Wiley and Sons, 1997), 295-96.

2   Chris Fontanella, *Jump-Start Your Career: Ten Tips to Get You Going* (Littleton, CO: Illumify Media Global, 2022), 56.

3   *Network*, written by Paddy Chayefsky, directed by Sidney Lumet, produced by Howard Gottfried (Metro-Goldwyn-Mayer, 1976), https://www.scriptslug.com/script/network-1976.

4   Francesca Gino, *Rebel Talent: Why It Pays to Break the Rules at Work and in Life* (New York: Harper Collins, 2018), 18.

5   Mark Manson, *The Subtle Art of Not Giving a F*ck: A Counterintuitive Approach to Living a Good Life* (New York: Harper Collins Publishers, 2016), 19.

6   Phil Knight, *Shoe Dog: A Memoir by the Creator of Nike* (New York: Scribner, 2016), 5.

7   Krista Williams, Malcolm Weir, and Lynn Buzhardt, "Can Old Dogs Learn New Tricks?" VCAHospitals.com, accessed October 9, 2024, https://vcahospitals.com/know-your-pet/can-old-dogs-learn-new-tricks#:~:text=Dispelling%20the%20myth,Dogs%20are%20innately%20good%20learners.

8   Mary Catherine Bateson, *Composing a Further Life* (New York: Knopf, 2010), 72, 181.

Chapter 3: An Appreciation of Variation

1   Kristen Bieler, "His Place in the Sun", *Wine Spectator Magazine*, May 31, 2023, 28.

2   Kristen Bieler, "His Place in the Sun," 29.

3   Kristen Bieler, "His Place in the Sun," 34.

4   Kristen Bieler, "His Place in the Sun," 34.

5   Kristen Bieler, "His Place in the Sun," 36.

6   Kristen Bieler, "His Place in the Sun," 36.

7   Quentin Crisp, *How to Have a Lifestyle* (New York: Methuen, 1975), 8.

8   *Jerry Maguire*, written by Cameron Crowe, (TriStar Pictures, 1996), imsdb.com/scripts/jerry-maguire.html.

9   *Harry Potter and the Goblet of Fire*, written by Steve Kloves, (Warner Bros, 2005), http://nldslab.soe.ucsc.edu/charactercreator/film_corpus/film_20100519/all_imsdb_05_19_10/Harry-Potter-and-the-Goblet-of-Fire.html.

10 Lewis Carroll, *Alice's Adventures in Wonderland and Through the Looking-Glass* (San Diego: Word Cloud Classics, 2016), 96.

11 Mary Catherine Bateson, *Composing a Further Life* (New York: Knopf, 2010), 92.

12 Duke, Annie. *Quit: The Power of Knowing When to Walk Away* (New York: Portfolio/Penguin, 2022), 213.

Chapter 4: Changing Lanes

1   Matt Craig, "Snoop Dreams," *Forbes*, October/November 2024, 70.

2   Troy Hill, local sales manager at KOMO TV station, in email discussion with author, August 2024.

3   Thomas Moore, *A Life at Work* (New York: Broadway Books, 2008), 129.

4   Francesca Gino, *Rebel Talent* (New York: HarperCollins Publishers, 2018), 85.

5   Wes "Scoop" Nisker, *The Big Bang, the Buddha, and the Baby Boom: The Spiritual Experiments of My Generation* (San Francisco: HarperSanFrancisco, 2003), 73.

6   Armstrong, Karen, *Buddha* (New York: Penguin Putnam, 2001), 35.

Chapter 5: Stroll Down, Don't Park on Memory Lane

1   Steven Johnson, *Where Good Ideas Come From: The Natural History of Innovation* (New York: Riverhead Books, 2010), 35.

2   Bob Iger, *The Ride of a Lifetime: Lessons Learned From 15 Years as CEO of the Walt Disney Company* (New York: Random House, 2019), 9.

3   Lamott, Anne. *Almost Everything: Notes on Hope* (New York: Riverhead Books, 2018), 158.

Chapter 6: Career Mechanics Inspect the Mechanics

1   "Righter's Auto Repair, "Five Common Problems with Classic Cars You Should Expect," December 15, 2020, http://rightersautorepair.com/5-common-problems-with-classic-cars-you-should-expect/.

2   Aldous Huxley, "Over-Organization" in *Brave New World Revisited* (New York: Harperperennial Modern Classics, 2004), 251.

3   Anna Helhoski, "Tech Layoffs 2024: Layoffs Hit Apple, Redfin," nerdwallet.com, updated August 29, 2024, https://www.nerd-wallet.com/article/finance/tech-layoffs#.

4   "Outsourcing Advisory," KPMG.com, accessed October 10, 2024, https://kpmg.com/us/en/capabilities-services/advisory-services/procurement/outsourcing-advisory.html.

Chapter 7: Hand Me a Wrench

[1] Arianna Huffington, *Thrive: The Third Metric to Redefining Success and Creating a Life of Well-Being, Wisdom, and Wonder* (New York: Harmony Books, 2015), 2.

[2] Arianna Huffington, *Thrive*, 22.

[3] Arianna Huffington, *Thrive*, 38.

[4] Arianna Huffington, *Thrive*, 155.

[5] Tom Rath and Donald O. Clifton, *How Full Is Your Bucket: Positive Strategies for Work and Life* (New York: Gallup Press, 2004), 15.

[6] Tom Rath and Donald O. Clifton, *How Full Is Your Bucket,* 53.

[7] Tess Vigeland, *Leap: Leaving a Job with No Plan B to Find the Career and Life You Really Want* (New York: Harmony Books, 2015), 125.

[8] Susan Cain, *Quiet: The Power of Introverts in a World That Can't Stop Talking* (New York: Random House, 2012), 219.

[9] Barbara Mitchell, "Stepping Down the Ladder," The Center for Association Leadership, accessed October 11, 2022, https://www.asacenter.org/association-careerhq/career/articles/job-search-strategies/stepping-back-down-the-ladder.

[10] Lewis Carroll, *Alice's Adventures in Wonderland and Through the Looking-Glass* (San Diego: Canterbury Classics, 2016), 49.

[11] Anna Quindlen, *A Short Guide to a Happy Life* (New York: Random House, 2000), 16.

[12] Anna Quindlen, A Short Guide to a Happy Life, 16.

[13] Stephen M. Pollan and Mark Levine, *Die Broke: A Radical, Four-Part Financial Plan to Restore Your Confidence, Increase Your Net Worth, and Afford You the Lifestyle of Your Dreams* (New York: HarperBusiness,1997), 26.

[14] Alan Briskin, *The Stirring of the Soul in the Workplace* (San Francisco: Jossey-Bass, 1996), 143.

[15] Sam Keen, *Fire in the Belly* (New York: Bantam Books, 1992), 61.

[16] Rick Rubin, *The Creative Act: A Way of Being* (New York: Penguin Press, 2023), 161.

[17] *Days of Thunder,* written by Robert Towne and Tom Cruise, directed by Tony Scott (Don Simpson/Jerry Bruckheimer Films, 1990), https://www.scripts.com/script/days_of_thunder_6450#google_vignette.

Conclusion

[1] *The Intern*, written and directed by Nancy Meyers (Warner Bros, 2015), https://www.scripts.com/script/the_intern_20530.

ABOUT THE AUTHOR

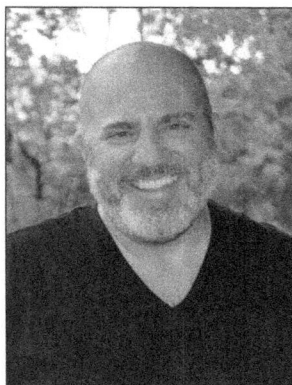

THE AUTHOR OF FOUR BOOKS on career advice, Chris Fontanella began adulthood working with nonprofits before transitioning into the staffing and consulting industry. He then founded Encore Professionals Group, a firm that specializes in placing accounting and finance professionals in temporary and full-time positions. He lives in Glendora, California, with his wife, Stacey.

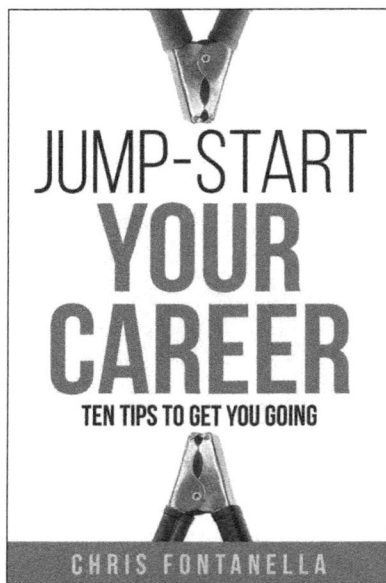

Look under the hood before it's too late and learn to

- Take ownership of your career.
- Consider entrepreneurship.
- Take a broader view of "wrong" moves.
- Realize a step down can be a step up.

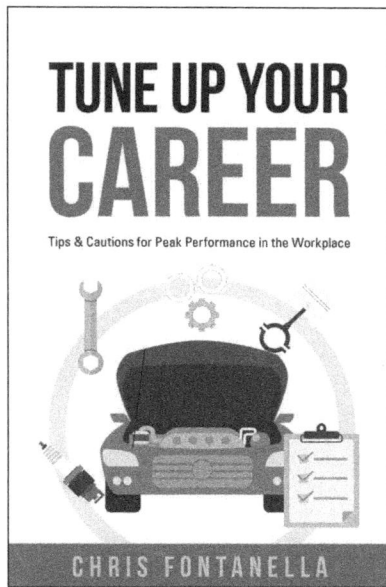

TUNE UP YOUR CAREER

Tips & Cautions for Peak Performance in the Workplace

CHRIS FONTANELLA

This is a guidebook to help shape who you are as a person, which in turn can shape your career. You'll learn how to

- Identify the overarching theme that gives your life meaning
- Map out your career by finding your "area of exploration"
- Abandon inconsequential goals
- Concentrate more on getting the job done and less on getting credit